The Complete History

of **Parkside**

Buffalo, NY

By Steve Cichon

ISBN 978-0-615-32784-6

First Printing: November, 2009

Second Printing: December, 2009

Third Printing, with correction of typographical errors: January, 2010

Contents

The Parkside Area- Courtesy Google Maps

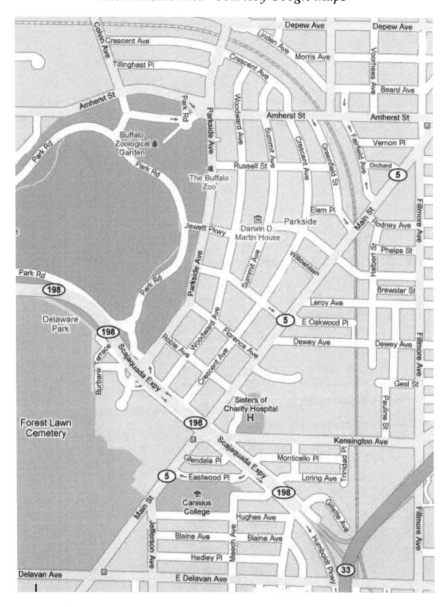

The Frederick Law Olmsted designed Parkside neighborhood runs from Humboldt Parkway north to the NYCRR tracks, and from Parkside Avenue west to Main Street. The Parkside Community Association also serves The Burbank Terrace area on the other side of the 198, and the "Vernon Triangle," east of the railroad tracks and west of Main Street.

Preface

To North Buffalonians and the people of Kenmore, Parkside is the road to get to and from the Kensington Expressway. To Western New Yorkers at large, it's "where we park for free when we go to the zoo." To out-of-towners, it might be best known as the home of one of Frank Lloyd Wright's finest works. But even most of the residents who dwell within the boundaries of the neighborhood don't fully know and appreciate the varied and rich history of the area they call home.

This volume is called "The Complete History of Parkside," but is meant only as a starting place. To date, no where else in one volume would you have been able to read in any great detail about the War of 1812, Frank Lloyd Wright, EB Green, Sisters Hospital, Frederick Law Olmsted, the Zoo, street cars, The Ford Motor Company, and all of the dozens of other interesting and varied topics that coalesce to provide such a textured and deep history as the Parkside story.

It's my great hope that this "Complete History" becomes a jumping off point for more stories and photos and lore to be remembered and shared, not just of Parkside, but its institutions and surrounding neighborhoods as well.

A few words about this book: In many cases, historical volumes are quoted directly. As a lover of not only history, but the English language, I can't help but share directly the style and flavor provided in many accounts written by those who actually experienced these historical events. I also only provide cursory facts where there is already an abundance of information readily available. There are many great books, for example, on Frederick Law Olmsted and Frank Lloyd Wright. Very important people in Parkside's history, but to clutter these pages with information that's only a quick Google search away seems senseless and repetitive.

Finally, there are very few conclusions drawn by *me* in this book. In the later chapters of this book, there are several subjects covered about which some readers may still have very strong feelings or *open wounds*. Your comments are welcomed for Volume II.

Steve Cichon, September 2009

sjcichon@aol.com

Chapter 1: When Parkside was the Rugged Frontier

Long before European men tread through what is today known as Parkside, portions of the area were sacred to the Seneca Nation and their fellow members of the Haudenosaunee (Iroquois) League of Indian Nations. One legend passed down through the family of early resident Erastus Granger spins the tale that native chieftains would convene "Councils in the Oaks" on ancient battlefield here, destined to become part of the Granger property. When Granger became the area's first permanent resident in 1804, vast wilderness was all the eye could see. Later, his son Warren built a magnificent home, what generations of Parksiders called "The Castle," on the spot where native chiefs had met long before the scribes of modern history were there to record them.

The Granger Castle. Now the site of the Forest Lawn Sundial, Main St.

Today, the area is Forest Lawn Cemetery, and this specific plot is marked with a large sundial, easily visible from Main Street. Warren's daughter Anna Granger wrote of it:

> *When Warren Granger selected the situation to build his home, he fixed*
> *upon the spot where the "Six Nations" held their counsels, the elevation was*

crowned by a grand old oak. This part of Flint Hill was sacred to the Indians, for here many, many, many moons beyond the memory of the oldest chief, a fierce battle had been fought. The plow shares continually turned up skulls, arrow heads and tomahawks of ancient design.

There are also many early accounts of children finding bone fragments and arrowheads in massive quantities as they played in the woods along what is now Main Street. It was from the "Old Iroquois Forest," as the woods along Main Street in the Parkside area were known, that many of the logs were hewn to build the early structures of Buffalo; many more were used after the village was burned by the British in 1813.

In the 1790's, Western New York was bought from Massachusetts by Oliver Phelps and Nathaniel Gorham, defaulted on, and then purchased by Robert Morris. He was the financier of the American Revolution and, at the time of the purchase in 1791, the richest man in America. Over the next two years, he sold the land to The Holland Land Company. Before that transaction could be completed, however, peace had to be made with the Six Nations, the Indians who actually inhabited the area. That peace was accomplished with the 1797 Treaty of Big Tree, which called for 1,300,000 acres of Native land to be sold for $100,000; leaving the Seneca Nation with a 200,000 acre reservation, to the south of the tiny village of Buffalo. Seneca Chief Red Jacket was paid a $600 bonus at the signing, and was guaranteed $100 a year for the rest of his life. The Holland Land Company, under Joseph Elliott, began surveying the area today known as Western New York. It is this survey that is the starting point for most property deeds in the area, including in Parkside.

The first traces of modern Parkside are etched onto the map in 1797 when what is now Main Street is cut through the wilderness, connecting outposts in Clarence and Williamsville with the burgeoning village at the mouth of the Buffalo Creek. That village was officially known as New Amsterdam, but almost from the beginning known to locals as Buffaloe (yes, with an "e" in the early years).

Early Settlers

While many of the earliest residents of Parkside may have been Senecas, their names long forgotten to history; the names of the earliest white settlers still live on in file cabinets and safety deposit boxes. Many of the following names will be familiar to any Parkside homeowner who has read his or her property deed.

Erastus Granger was a central figure in the founding of Buffalo. He was among Buffalo's first permanent residents, and also the first Parkside Landowner who actually lived here as well. Having spent the early part of his life as a land speculator in Ohio, Kentucky and Western Virginia, he was to become an active supporter of the Democratic-Republican Party, and specifically of Thomas Jefferson. It was upon Jefferson's appointment Granger came to Buffalo in 1804. He purchased a vast tract of land along Main Street that stretched from what is now Forest Lawn Cemetery, north to the Delaware Park Meadow; and as far west as what is now the H.H. Richardson State Hospital Complex on Forest Avenue. His homestead was built along Conjockety's (now Scajaquada) Creek near Main Street. The area where his home stood is now the northern-most portion of Forest Lawn Cemetery, near the Canisius College campus.

Erastus Granger's home along Conjockety's (Scajaquada) Creek. Around 1915, Scajaquada Creek was covered starting at Main Street, running under Main Street near Jefferson Avenue.

Granger's life was written about at great length in the *Buffalo Sunday Express*, November 24, 1912. He was born January 17, 1765, in Suffield, Connecticut. As a boy, he spent part of the winter of 1777-78 encamped with the Continental Army with his father at Valley Forge. As a young man, eager for adventure, he became a surveyor of frontier lands. It was on his travels in Western Virginia in 1798-99 that he became acquainted with Thomas Jefferson, who prevailed upon Granger and his brother Gideon to campaign for him for President in their native Connecticut. Once Jefferson was elected, Gideon was named Postmaster General. Erastus was named Indian Agent for the Six Nations, and was also confirmed by the United States Senate as the "surveyor of the port of Buffalo creek."

He reached Buffalo Creek on horseback March 30, 1804, finding a frontier village of 16 huts, and the streets strewn with tree stumps. He quickly organized a post office. This handled the incoming mail, once a week, as a single horseman "came from Canandaigua with a pair of saddlebags and the trifling mail," and once a week he returned from Fort Niagara. Within three years of his arrival, in 1807, he was appointed as the outpost's first Judge.

Granger's most important work came, though, as Indian Agent. He met often with the great chiefs of the Six Nations, shared his harvests with them, and allowed them to continue to use his land on *Flint Hill* for their councils in the oaks.

"Flint Hill" was the name given to the Granger property and its immediate environs; well outside the boundaries of the then small village of Buffalo, about 4 miles to the north. Granger himself used the name "Flint Hill" to describe his home, but, by 1914, the name had so long fallen out of use that readers of *Peace Episodes on the Niagara* (Buffalo Historical Society) needed an explanation of the location of the place:

"Flint Hill" is a name little known to the present generation; but their elders in Buffalo knew it as the region mostly west of Main street and north of Humboldt Parkway, embracing most of the Parkside district and the adjacent portion of Delaware Park.

The first book ever published in Buffalo was a collection of public speeches given by Granger and his great friend, the Seneca Chief Red Jacket, made as war was declared between Great Britain and the United States. Both men spoke of the desire to keep the Six Nations neutral in the conflict which would become known to history as the War of 1812.

Red Jacket, Cornplanter, Farmer's Brother and other brilliant chiefs of the Seneca, Onondaga, Cayuga, Tuscarora and Oneida tribes were present on July 6, 1812, just days after word of war had reached Buffalo, when Judge Granger first offered a message of goodwill and friendship to the Indians, then spoke these words to the assembled council of Native Chiefs:

Your great father, the president of the 17 fires (James Madison), *now gives his red children the same advice which he gave you at the beginning of the last war* (the Revolution); *that is you take no part in the quarrels of the white people. He stands in no need of your assistance. His warriors are numerous, like sands on the shore of the great lake which cannot be counted. He is able to fight his own battles, and requests you stay home.*

The Six Nations would stay out of the conflict until the Mohawks, who had fled to Canada after the Revolution, joined on the side of the British.

Plains Rangers

Just north of Granger along Main Street was the area known as "The Buffalo Plains;" its inhabitants known as "The Plains Rangers." This wily group of frontiersmen-- most of them veterans of the Revolutionary War-- and their families settled and built farms along Main Street. Their homes were generally close to the Buffalo-Williamsville Road, or *the main street*, but like Granger, their farmlands extended as much as a mile or more to the east or west off Main Street.

These hard working, rough and tumble men cut from the wilderness the area that would become Parkside, Central Park, and the University District, and were the first white men to physically live within the current boundaries of those districts. They were respected, but also somewhat feared by the residents of the village several miles to the south. Barton Atkins described them this way in his 1898 book *Modern Antiquities: Sketches of Early Buffalo,* "On Buffalo Plains were resident a band of stalwart men noted for their prowess and of their proneness to assert it when the occasion offered."

The son of an original "Ranger," Atkins wrote of the initial settlement by the Rangers:

> *The Plains were originally settled by a colony of farmers from the lake region of Central New York. First to come on a tour of inspection was Samuel Atkins, in 1806, on horseback, traversing Indian trails through a dense forest to Buffalo -- not to speculate in village lots, but to purchase farm lands for himself and others who desired to settle near unto the site of the great city that was to arise at the foot of Lake Erie.*

Samuel Atkins built a log home and a tavern on the land he purchased, on Main Street north of Hertel Avenue, roughly where the LaSalle Metro Rail station stands today. Again writes Atkins:

> *On this property, in 1807, Mr. Atkins erected a majestic structure of logs, consisting of three separate buildings, made so by two dividing passages through the lower story, while the upper story and roof remained intact. The building entire was eighteen by eighty feet on the ground with side thirteen feet high -- quite an imposing frontier establishment. Here Mr. Atkins kept a tavern, a house of entertainment for travelers and pilgrims journeying to the new West. Many veterans of the war of the Revolution had settled on the*

*Niagara frontier, and the old log tavern was their headquarters-- was where
they held their camp-fires and fought their battles anew.*

Atkins was joined in 1807 by eight Cayuga County neighbors and
their families, including Rowland Cotton, Ephraim Brown and Roswell
Hosford. In 1808, the families of Zachary Griffin and Dr. Daniel Chapin also
came to Buffalo. All of these men and their families settled along Main
between Granger and what is now the UB area, both on the east and west
sides of Main Street.

Ephraim Brown was the oldest of the new settlers of the Buffalo
Plains. The war-worn veteran of the Revolution, cane in hand, was a favorite
of the youngsters on the Plains. He'd limp along with school children, as the
youngsters would gather at his knee-- a knee shattered by a musket ball at
the Battle of Trenton. They'd hear "Old Mr. Brown" sing, tell stories of his
battles, and chant army rhymes from colonial times. Brown's homestead
and farm where described by Barton Atkins as "opposite the County
Almshouse." The Erie County Almshouse moved in 1909, and the University
of Buffalo was built on the land.

Zachary Griffin's home survived well into the 20th century, and
would have been known to the earliest residents of Parkside- as we know it
today- as a part of their neighborhood. The following was written in *Peace
Episodes on the Niagara* (Buffalo Historical Society, 1914), about the home on
the east side of Main Street.

*In January, 1915, the
oldest house in Buffalo
was torn down. This
was a little one-story
structure at No. 2485
Main street, which
according to such
credible witnesses as
the late Washington
Russell and Barton
Atkins, was built in
1809 by Zachary
Griffin. When the*
*New York Central Belt Line Tracks were laid through the district the house as moved
about 100 feet northerly from its original site. Probably all of the original structure
that endured was the frame of heavy hewn timbers. The story goes that it was spared*

at the burning of Buffalo, in 1813, because the Indians, by the time they had got as far out as this on the Williamsville road, were too much overcome by firewater to do any further harm.

The original site of the house was about opposite Greenfield Street, and when moved, it was about where the Central Park Grill is located. The frontage of the property was split roughly in half when the New York Railroad Beltline tracks were installed in the 1870s. Next door, was the home of the widow Anna Atkins. She moved closer to the Modern Parkside area in 1817 after the death of her husband Samuel. That means that Barton Atkins, whose works are quoted throughout this history, was among the first children to be born and grow up in the current confines of Parkside.

Captain Rowland Cotton is the other *Plains Ranger* who owned a large portion of what is today Parkside. He owned the farm just to the north of present Jewett Parkway, and the homestead of Daniel Chapin. Cotton, too, was a Revolutionary War veteran, and was one of only three of the original Plains Rangers who did not make Buffalo home until their death. Cotton sold his plot in 1826, and settled in the Town of Lancaster. His name appears the deeds of those in the northern half of Parkside.

Dr. Daniel Chapin

The most notable Plains Rangers to the people of Parkside, are the ones who once owned the land upon which they now live. Dr. Daniel Chapin was a veteran of the Revolution, and lived in a log cabin, which was built at what is now the corner of Main Street and Jewett Parkway. His property bordered Erastus Granger, and was still considered part of the *Flint Hill* area. His property stretched along Main Street from what is now roughly West Oakwood Place to Jewett Parkway. It stretched back to encompass the southern half of the Delaware Park Meadow, and reached to the fringes of the Park (now Hoyt) Lake.

In the early years, Chapin was one of a very few medical doctors anywhere on the Niagara Frontier, and like his neighbor Granger, he was an early pillar of the community. An obituary was published in the *Rochester Telegraph* December 4, 1821:

> *He was formerly from Salisbury, Ct. He represented the county of Ontario in the legislature of this state, very soon after that county was settled; and was an early settler of this county. He had held the office of judge of common pleas for Niagara county* (that is, Buffalo, before Erie County was split

off); *and various public trusts, with benefit to the community. His reputation as a physician, during a long course of practice has been of honorable standing; and he lived and died an honest man.*

Chapin can also be thanked for much of the natural beauty today enjoyed in Delaware Park. His love of nature was written about in the Historical Society's First Volume on Buffalo History:

The people of this city are much indebted to the Doctor, who was one of the pioneers of Buffalo, for the good taste and judgment exercised in clearing up his farm. Coming on to it in 1806, and ever having an eye to the beauty of native scenery and landscape, he left and always preserved with care, groups and scattered trees of various sizes and kinds, where it would add to its beauty; and we in our park enjoy the benefit of his sentiment and forbearance. He was imbued with the idea of the poet who says, "Woodman, spare that tree;' and when he could, he always had trees left untouched by the ruthless axe, in order that man and beast should benefit by their shade, and they with their primitive grace ornament his beautiful farm. His son, the late Col. William W. Chapin, always protected and preserved those trees with truly reverential and pious care, in memory of and respect for his honored father, who left the inheritance of the whole farm to him on his decease. Without that inherited taste, he, like most of the early settlers, would have denuded the land of every tree; and that portion of our park would have been a barren expanse of mere farming land; for a large portion of this old farm now constitutes the most interesting part of our beautiful park. As one rides through it, especially that portion I speak of, he cannot help noticing those groups of trees and scattered monarchs of the forest within and on the borders of the extensive Park Meadow; beautiful reminders of those thoughtful and tasteful former proprietors.

An important historical figure in the Finger Lakes area as well as Parkside, he is written about by the Bloomfield Historical Society:

Dr. Daniel came to Buffalo village in 1807 from Bloomfield, put up a log house on the outskirts of the village, and established a large practice, visiting his patients on foot, with a dog and a gun, often traveling trails as far as Niagara Falls. Dr. Chapin died in 1821 at 60, his death due to exposure in visiting a patient.

The varied accounts of Chapin's death all point to the difficult life on the frontier north of Buffalo. The obituary from the *Rochester Telegraph*, which states it was reprinted from a Buffalo paper, says Chapin was 61 and died of "a lingering disease." Another source, *A Biographical Sketch of Josiah Trowbridge* (1869), he another early Buffalo doctor, states that Chapin's death was "partly induced by the many and continued exposures incident to the practice of his profession in times when it required an amount of personal courage, self-denial, and hardship but little understood by us of the present day."

Chapter 2: Parkside Goes to War

Erastus Granger had been at Flint Hill less than a decade; the Plains Rangers less than five years when the War of 1812 broke out. The Parkside/Flint Hill area played several prominent roles in that conflict. Flint Hill was an encampment and training ground for soldiers preparing to invade Canada. It was also a sanctuary when the village of Buffalo was burned to the ground. Given the nature of war and brutal Buffalo winters, the area also served as a burial ground for hundreds who never made it home.

Throughout much of the documentation about the War of 1812, the Flint Hill Camp was described as "Camp near Buffalo." This was explained in *Peace Episodes on the Niagara* (Buffalo Historical Society, 1914). "In 1812, the Army of the Frontier went into winter quarters at Flint Hill, with Scajaquada creek as a convenient water supply." Barton Atkins, the great chronicler of history of this period, wrote about the encampment in *Modern Antiquities*:

> The camp extended on Main Street from the present Humboldt Parkway
> northerly to the lands of Dr. Daniel Chapin... and westerly to the head of
> the Park Lake, on lands belonging to Erastus Granger. On the Main-street
> front of this old camp-ground stand several venerable oaks, relics of the old
> camp. The one directly opposite the Deaf and Dumb Asylum is
> distinguished as the one under which a row of soliders kneeled when shot
> for desertion in the spring of 1813.

The camp spread from what is now Forest Lawn to near Jewett Parkway along Main Street, and stretched as far back as the Delaware Park Lake. The shooting mentioned was Buffalo's first execution. As of 1914, one of the old trees that bore witness to the capital punishment still remained in the backyard of 24 Florence Avenue (corner of Crescent.)

Flint Hill, along with the rest of the Niagara Frontier, was a hotbed of activity early in the war as a planned launching point for the invasion of British Canada, and as it was Indian Agent Granger's job to keep the Native

Americans neutral. The Buffalo Gazette of June 2nd, 1812, reports Granger met with the chiefs of the Six Nations, at which time they acknowledged no desire to enter conflict between the US and Canada.

By early August however, after the rumor spread of the British and their Indian Allies gaining control of Seneca-owned Grand Island, Seneca chief Red Jacket told Granger that the Seneca Warriors wished to join the conflict against the British and "drive off those bad people from our land." As his correspondence from the time shows, Granger spent much of the ensuing year walking a tightrope, trying to make both the Indians and the powers in Washington happy.

The most complete meetings of chiefs in many years was held again on Main Street at the Granger farm in September, and this time the Senecas, the Onondagas, and the Cayugas voted to "take up the hatchet on behalf of the United States." Those who volunteered their services at the council agreed that they "would go home as soon as the council fire was extinguished, arm and equip themselves for battle, and return to Buffalo."

Though it was the continued hope to keep the young men of the Six Nations neutral, given the fact that "within a fortnight, between two and four hundred savages" would be in Buffalo ready to fight, President James Madison was forced to allow Granger to accept the services and organize the warriors of the Six Nations.

Still, there were many stops and starts in the Iroquois joining the war effort. Several times, after being asked to assemble, native warriors weren't used. After nearly a year of "dancing" between native chiefs and Washington bureaucrats, the two sides kept in alliance by the constant work of Granger, it was Granger's safety that ultimately had the Indians take to arms in combat.

They finally entered the conflict when their friend, Erastus Granger, was in peril. The Canadian British put a price on his head, and had Flint Hill... yes, modern day Parkside... marked for destruction. Judge Granger received word of this on July 10, 1813, and sent word to the greatest Seneca warrior of his time, the old chief Farmer's Brother. Granger's longtime compatriot, who fought in both the French and Indian War of the 1760s, and the American War of Independence, had received a medal from George Washington for his service. It was also "from Washington's lips" that came the name "Farmer's Brother," by which the chief would be known for the rest of his days.

A man of at least 80 years old in 1813, Farmer's Brother traveled from his hut in the Indian village in today's South Buffalo, to what's now the Parkside neighborhood, with warriors in tow, ready to fight. The Indians readied for war at the Granger home on Main Street. James Granger wrote an account of the night in his 1893 book *Granger Genealogy.*

> *The chief and his followers arrived at 11 o'clock, and the night was spent preparing for the coming fray. Bullets were molded by the great fire in the kitchen* (of the Granger Homestead)*, messengers hurried into the neighboring village for arms and ammunition, and the Indians were banqueted on unlimited salt pork prepared by Mrs. Granger's own hands.*

After over a year of waiting to join the conflict, the Senecas would finally join the war. Granger, led by Farmer's Brother and the Senecas followed Guide Board Road (North Street today) to Black Rock. There, they met with General Porter, who decided to initiate an offensive against the British along the shores of the Niagara River.

The Senecas prepared for battle in a ritual never seen by the American troops assembled at the spot. They took of all of their clothes; stripped down to their breechcloths. Granger and the Senecas were on the right side of the line, regulars in the middle, white volunteers to the left, ready to take on the British. At the order of General Porter, the Indians leapt forward with a yell that startled both their enemy... *and* their allies. Within minutes, the enemy had retreated. The Indians had even rushed into the water to pull soldiers from their boats as they paddled in retreat for the safety of the Canadian shore. The victory was complete. Buffalo, Black Rock, and Granger's Flint Hill Estate were safe, for now, due mostly to the tenacity of Farmer's Brother's men.

Because of its location, both high in elevation, and a relatively safe-yet-close-enough distance to Black Rock, Flint Hill had become an important meeting place for the military leaders both the United States and of the Six Nations (now Five Nations, with the Mohawks fighting along side the British.) Captain George Howard of the 25th Infantry spent some time at the Granger place recovering his strength and health. He wrote home to Connecticut on June 6, 1813, that he had met many of the famous chiefs of the Six Nations, including Red Jacket, Parrot Nose, Bill Johnson, Young King, Farmer's Brother, and Silver Heels.

The Burning of Buffalo

Five months after that first battle, in December, 1813, by now Col. Granger and 83 Seneca Warriors under his command again responded to a British attack on Black Rock, but this time, they were forced to retreat when so many other soldiers fled from the line. Granger returned to his home, several miles away, to relative safety. As hoards of men retreated, and the lines of protection broke apart, the British marched up Niagara Street from Black Rock to Buffalo, and over the course of the coming days, laid torch to all but a handful of buildings in the village of Buffalo.

As the British and their Indian allies made their way towards Buffalo, the women and children of the village moved north up Main Street in an obviously harried fashion. Though many fled as far as Clarence Hollow and Williamsville, many dozens sought refuge and stayed safe in the home of Judge Granger on Flint Hill, and in the homes of the Buffalo Plains. As mentioned in the previous chapter, it is noted in several histories, including *Studies of the Niagara Frontier,* that homes on the Buffalo Plains, like that of Zachary Griffin, were not burned because, "*the Indians in their course of destruction with musket and firebrand were too much overcome with liquor before they reached this house to do any further damage."*

In fact, none of the buildings as far north as current day Parkside were burned as the British and their Indian allies left Buffalo a pile of smoldering timber. It made the area, especially Granger's place, a location where many women and children took up semi-permanent residence, while the men who weren't taking to arms took to rebuilding the village.

Encampment at Buffalo

Picture Delaware Park, all along the Scajaquada Expressway, over the Park Meadow and golf course, all the way up to Main Street filled with tents, bonfires, and soldiers milling about. As early as September 1812, over a year before the burning of Buffalo, General Alexander Smythe had planned to use Buffalo and Black Rock as a staging ground for an invasion of Canada; many of his troops, particularly Pennsylvania volunteers under the command of General Adamson Tannehill, were camped and drilling at Flint Hill.

Smythe was an interesting character, if not an effective General, or even a buffoon. His actions (and inactions) make it apparent that he felt that inspirational writing and speeches could surmount instilling discipline and training his men, many of whom were not professional soldiers, but volunteers; signing up only as the Union was in peril. Smythe was written of by Frank Severance in *Episodes of Peace on the Niagara* (1914):

> *He was... often ridiculous, and has been remembered... chiefly because of certain bombastic proclamations which he issued during his short career in Buffalo and vicinity. Historians... have written of him only in a vein of amused contempt.... calling him "supercilious, dictatorial, impertinent."* (and) *"indecisive, puerile and cowardly."*

The folly and incompetence of General Smythe made his troops rambunctious. During the fall and winter of 1812, many citizens of the Buffalo area were alarmed to find their fields and barns being plundered by Smythe's hungry or simply bored soldiers. William Hodge, Jr. wrote about one series of incidents in *Recalling Pioneer Days:*

> *Once several fat sheep were put into a horse stable, among the horses, just at night to be dressed the next morning; but when morning came they were gone. They had been taken a short distance into the orchard, and dressed, or butchered and carried off to camp. At last some of the soldiers were caught at this work. They were taken to their camp, and delivered up to the officers for punishment; but to this the officers were not disposed. This rather exasperated some of the inhabitants, who asked the commanding officer what they should do to the soldiers if they were caught at any more of these depredations. He said, "Shoot them, shoot them down the rascals."*

> *After this a number of the young men of the town kept watch at night. Of this group Velorus Hodge was one and they kept watch one night at the bridge of Granger's creek, Main street.* (This is roughly the intersection of Main Street and Jefferson Avenue.) *After a while the one on guard outside discovered eight soldiers crossing the bridge, and hailed them. They answered, "What businesses have you to stop soldiers on the march?" and then a pistol was fired by one of them. The guard returned the fire. This started out those in the house; they sallied forth and all fired at the soldiers giving them an effectual peppering with shot.*

> *Five of the soldiers fell to the ground and three making their escape. Of the five four were wounded by the shot; the fifth fell to save himself from being shot. These five were marched into camp the next morning and delivered over to the commanding officer, who approved of the course taken by the citizens. This put a check upon the stealing and plundering for quite a while.*

Granger's Creek is today Scajaquada Creek. The bridge talked about, though well hidden, still goes over Main Street near Jefferson.

Plans to Invade Canada Hatched in Parkside

Plainly, his troops hated him. General Smythe wrote many verbose and bombastic proclamations to his troops, and verbally delivered several more, most of which won him "the derision of friend and foe." He was known as "Alexander the Great" and "Napoleon the Second." Plenty of his hot air was blown in preparation for his plans to invade Canada.

Those plans were set into motion on November 28, 1812. Smythe had as many as 8,000 men champing at the bit. He had been building, collecting, and fixing boats by the dozen for crossing the Niagara River at Black Rock. At this point, Smythe's rhetoric had worked, whipping his men into a frenzy, ready to spill across the river at Black Rock for *the glory of the union*. Trumpets played *Yankee Doodle Dandy*, further lighting the fires under the men on a cold winter day, with wind and snow blowing off the Niagara River. An early morning crossing of 420 men in 21 boats were met with musket fire as they approached the shore to the south of Fort Erie. What happened next was the final straw for Smythe's men. What happened… was nothing. Wrote Frank Severance in *Episodes of Peace on the Niagara* (1914):

> *From sunrise to late afternoon, his army was embarking- the enemy on the other side of the river, in constantly-increasing numbers, looking on at the show. General Smythe did not appear at all, leaving the details to his subordinates. For hours the troops shivered in the boats, some of which, stranded on shore, filled with snow and ice. Late in the day, when at length everything seemed ready for a grand movement across the stream, General Smythe issued an amazing order: "Disembark and dine!" Disgusted and angered, the whole force was at the point of rebellion.*

Two more days of similar commands to climb aboard boats… spend the day in the tiny wooden craft, freezing along the Niagara River shore in late November Buffalo weather, and then never leaving that snow and ice-filled shore.

After having been "whipped into a frenzy" days before, some men smashed their muskets against trees in disgust, and many of those who didn't ruin their guns made mutinous use of them, firing in the direction of Smythe himself. Legend has it that musket ball holes filled General Smythe's Flint Hill tent by the end of that third night. Of the 1700 Pennsylvania volunteers camped at Flint Hill, 600 deserted in a 24 hour period. General Peter Porter wrote an article in the *Buffalo Gazette* calling Smythe a coward for refusing to move forward with the planned invasion. The two fought a duel with pistols, but both shots were errant, neither hitting the other.

Between his officer colleague and the angry soldiers under his command, Smythe had survived perhaps dozens attempts on his life over a two week period, and had had enough. On December 17, 1812, within days of his *three* failed attempts at invading Canada, and, fresh on the heels of gun fire pointed in his direction from both a fellow general and his own men, Smythe would leave Buffalo and Flint Hill for his native Virginia. The Army Register states that he was "disbanded."

But the soldiers who lived through the rest of the winter of 1813 on Flint Hill had not yet seen the worst of it all. A horrific lasting monument to the war, still in Parkside, but little known, had yet to be created.

Buffalo's Tomb of the Unknowns

Enlist your imagination once again. Picture living in Buffalo, in November and December, in open-ended tents, wearing linen uniforms, and having only very few, if any, blankets, coats, socks and boots. It was these conditions in Parkside in 1813 that yielded the mass, virtually unmarked grave that thousands of Western New Yorkers unknowingly drive by each day as they commute by Delaware Park on Route 198.

Up until the time of Smythe's abortive campaign to invade, the mostly Southern soldiers all lived in mere pup tents. In Buffalo. In the winter. Once the offensive proved a failure, they were ordered to build huts for the winter, but most were slow to comply. The troops stationed on Flint Hill were mostly from Pennsylvania, and even further south, and showed up to Buffalo, in autumn, in their linen uniforms. Now winter had arrived, but more appropriate uniforms had not. Many Buffalo, Flint Hill, and Buffalo Plains families took in soldiers, but the village was just too small to accommodate the great number of troops wintering here.

Food supplies were unreliable to the front in Buffalo, and food that arrived was often rancid. Colonel Widner, Smythe's second in command, stationed at Fort Niagara, had been experiencing the same conditions to the north. He reported in a letter to his commander in at Flint Hill, "We're starving at this end of the line for bread." The conditions were same at the camp that ran through what is now Forest Lawn Cemetery, along Main

Street to the north, and into Delaware Park.

It is among these demoralized, starving, freezing troops that a "Camp Distemper," described as a "dreadful contagion" broke out. The following account comes from an American prisoner of the British, and pays eyewitness account to what the winter of 1812-13 was like in Parkside:

> *That the enemy have about 3,000 troops one mile and a half in rear of Black Rock, under camp at a place called Judge Granger's, where the General (Smythe), his aide-de-camp and several officers of rank live.. their camp is unhealthy... they die from eight to nine daily... the dead.. are put into holes two or three of which are made every day, and into each put two to four dead men. The doctors say the disease is as bad as the plague. The patients are first taken with a pain in the head, and in an hour-and-a-half or two hours they invariably die. Besides this disease he mentions their being afflicted with pleurisy, dysentery, and measles.*

The Buffalo newspapers of the day daily listed the names of the dead, until the numbers became too great; eventually the Army stopped releasing the names. The home towns, listed next to the names, show, once again, that these men, from places like Baltimore, southern Pennsylvania, and Virginia, would have likely had a difficult time acclimating to Buffalo's winter climate, even without the starvation and disease that was present. From the *Buffalo Gazette*, on December 22, 1812:

> *The FEVER, which has made such dreadful havoc among our soldiers and citizens, continues to rage. The Physicians are taking unwearied pains to ascertain the character of the disease and to prescribe an effective remedy for it. Bloodletting is generally fatal in violent cases.*

It wasn't just soldiers who contracted this illness. While the causes of many of their deaths are lost to history, it's a fact that many residents of the Buffalo Plains and Flint Hill died during this time. Among those who passed that winter were Samuel Atkins, the first Plains Ranger, and Parthenia Chapin, the wife of Dr. Daniel Chapin.

Whether Mrs. Chapin died from one of the many illnesses sweeping through the camp or not, it is certain that she knew of the suffering first hand. It was on the outskirts of the Chapin property that the several daily shallow graves mentioned above were dug. As any gardener in Parkside knows, Flint Hill derives its name from the rocky soil abundant in the area. This is also apparent to anyone who drives the Kensington Expressway; and sees the solid rock that was blasted through near the Scajaquada Expressway interchange.

While digging graves by hand would be a challenge in good weather, these graves, again two or three per day, were being dug in the difficult frozen ground of winter. Often times, they were no more than a foot deep. Dr. Chapin offered his land for the burial, and tavern owner William Hodge was pressed into service to make coffins for the dead. Records say he crafted 300 pine coffins to be used for burying the soldiers who died while encamped on Flint Hill. Written in *Buffalo Cemeteries* (1879):

> *The troops of General Smythe remained at Flint Hill until the following spring. During this time there prevailed among them a typhoid epidemic. Deprived as they were of comfortable hospitals, and a sufficient supply of medical agents, it carried off about three hundred of them. They were put into plain pine board coffins, furnished by William Hodge Sr., and temporarily buried near the south line of the Chapin place; but the rock came so near to the surface that their graves could not be more than about a foot in depth.*

> *The ensuing spring they were removed some distance, to the north side of the farm, where the ground was a sandy loam and easily dug. Leave to bury them there being given by the respective owners of the farms, Capt. Rowland Cotton and Doctor Daniel Chapin, they were deposited directly on the dividing line between these farms, in one common grave. Doctor Chapin planted two yellow willows, one at each end of the grave, which have become large trees, and are yet growing. The grave itself remaining undisturbed to this day.*

The grave was to be known in coming years as "The Mound in the Meadow," with those willows coming from clippings of a yellow willow taken from Daniel Chapin's yard. The willows lasted on the site until at least 1896, when on July 4th; a boulder was placed on the site of the grave, with a marker attached.

It's worthy to note that among those dead might not only be US soldiers, but perhaps servants who died while attending to the sick, and perhaps even prisoners of war- Canadian and British being held captive who met the same horrible fate as the Americans.

The boulder and the remains of roughly 300 souls are still buried below the park meadow, in the middle of what is now the Delaware Park Golf Course inside Ring Road.

The marker reads: To the memory of the unnamed soldiers of the War of 1812 who died of camp disease and were buried here.

Aside from the boulder in the middle of the golf course, the mass grave of 300 American Soldiers, fallen in wartime service, goes unmarked, and unremembered, having been largely ignored for the last 100 years. Plans to properly mark the spot and honor the dead have come and gone over the last two centuries; you'll read of those plans as the story continues.

As the spring of 1813 broke, and Chapin and Cotton were giving proper burial to the dead, some of those soldiers who had survived the horrible winter began to think pacifist thoughts, and wanted to leave while the getting was good. The commanding officers made an example of several soldiers who tried to desert. As a previously included account spells out, these deserters were knelt in a row and shot in front of several oak trees along Main Street near, generally near what is today Florence Avenue. Their bodies were then hanged from the trees to dissuade any further desertion from the ranks at Flint Hill.

Troops Return to Flint Hill

As the War of 1812 raged on into 1813, and then 1814, a much more well-organized effort to invade British Canada was hatched. A year after the bungled attempts just outlined, some of the soldiers poised to invade Fort Erie made their pre-attack camp once again in what is now Forest Lawn Cemetery, Delaware Park, and the Parkside neighborhood.

In the spring of 1814, the more successful plan to invade Upper Canada was devised by a man, unlike General Smythe, who was a master tactician. Brigadier General Winfield Scott would lead his men to victory just over the Niagara River in the Battle of Chippawa; many joining the battle from their home base on Flint Hill. Scott, known to his men as *Ol' Fuss and Feathers*, on account of his insistence upon military appearance and discipline, later wrote books on infantry tactics, exercises, and maneuvers that are still used by the US Army to this day. Many of these formation schemes and tactics were first devised as Scott prepared for battles such as the one at Chippawa. It's therefore natural to assume the drills and discipline that would emerge as the foundation for the teaching done at West Point were first practiced by "the man who wrote the book," in staging grounds and base camps like the Delaware Park Meadow.

Chapter 3: Peace in the Country

Once peace was made, life slowed down considerably in the outlying area that was the Flint Hill/Parkside area; still 4-and-a-half miles north of the action of the village of Buffalo. And plenty of action there was. Through much political wrangling, the Village of Buffalo was selected as the terminus of the Erie Canal in 1825, bypassing the village of Black Rock, and sealing Buffalo's fate as a major player in trade for the next century.

North Street (as the name implies) was the city's northern border when it incorporated as a city in 1832. And even after Main Street was *Macadamized*, a rudimentary form of paving, in 1839, the ride along "the Main Road" between Buffalo and Williamsville, through the Parkside area, was still a bumpy ride through *"the country."*

Just as today, it was thought one way to solve the city's problems was through taxes. The collection of tolls paid for the improvements to the Buffalo-Williamsville Road; dozens of toll gates were erected from Buffalo to

Schardt's Tavern, which was on the southeast corner of Steele and Main, served as a "halfway house," a rest stop between Buffalo and Williamsville back in a day when travel was more difficult and time consuming.

Albany long the stretch, including one adjacent to Schardt's tavern at Main and Steele Streets.

Steele was later to be renamed Kensington Avenue, and later Humboldt Parkway would cut through the corner, meaning Buffalo's first toll booth was roughly at the corner of what is now Main and Humboldt.

Many of the men who first came to occupy what is now Parkside were well into middle age when they came here in the first decade of the 1800s. Therefore, by the 1820s and 1830s, many of the original pioneers were giving way to a new generation, many of whom knew *Flint Hill* and the *Buffalo Plains* as their only home.

Warren Granger

Judge Erastus Granger would retire most of his public offices, and live out his final years at Flint Hill; his 700 acres scattered with homes for friends and family members. He remained a firm Republican, and a close friend of New York Governor DeWitt Clinton. He was one of many Buffalonians who pushed for the building of the Erie Canal, and pushed for its western terminus to be located in Buffalo.

His friendship with Red Jacket also grew. Granger was buried on Christmas Day, 1826. Following the funeral, as the casket was about to be lowered into the grave, Red Jacket stood forward, and stared intently upon the face of the deceased. The great Indian Chief then delivered in his native Seneca tongue a final eulogy and prayer for his close friend. Those who heard it and understood it, said it was one of Red Jacket's finest oratories, in a career of fine oratory. The

It's so much an integral part of Buffalo's early history, a ceremony wherein Red Jacket gave Erastus Granger a ceremonial tomahawk is a part of the frieze on the face of Buffalo City Hall on the Elmwood Avenue side.

men's friendship was legendary enough to be etched on the façade of City Hall.

In 1845, Erastus's son Warren Granger built for himself a great stone mansion on the site of the ancient Councils in the Oaks of the Senecas. Again, this place is now marked at Forest Lawn Cemetery by a large sundial, easily visible from Main Street. *(See Photo on Page 5 and below.)*

The Gothic Structure was designed by Calvin Otis, built by John Ambrose, and made of stone quarried from the estate. It was destined to become the center of the Buffalo social scene, despite it's out of the way location. Like his father before him, Warren was a staunch Republican. His home saw parties during the Hard Cider campaign of William Henry Harrison, and actually played host to then-former President John Quincy Adams in 1848. And there is scarcely a doubt that Granger was in attendance when Abraham Lincoln stopped in Buffalo in February 1861 on his way to Washington to take the oath of office as President.

The Granger's property was considered among the most beautiful on the Niagara Frontier, and, in 1850, the Granger Family sold most of its vast tracts of rolling green acreage to the City of Buffalo. Some of it, 80 acres worth, was destined to become Forest Lawn Cemetery. But the rest of the land, including Granger's quarry and his meadow, would be reserved by the City for future use as a park. It would be over a quarter of a century, however, before Frederick Law Olmsted would unveil plans to transform the areas raw, natural beauty into the Delaware Park we know today.

Washington Adams Russell

Captain Rowland Cotton was one of the original Plains Rangers, and was the Revolutionary War veteran who helped Daniel Chapin exhume and re-inter the 300 souls who died at the Flint Hill camp in 1813. He moved to the village of Lancaster in 1826, and as those Parksiders who live between

Jewett Parkway and Russell Avenue will note on their property deeds, Cotton sold his farm to Washington Adams Russell.

Russell was the son of James Russell, a Revolutionary War Captain who happened to be well acquainted with the Commander-In-Chief of the Continental Army, George Washington. When Russell's son was born in 1801, he named him after the first two Presidents of the United States — George Washington and John Adams.

Washington Adams Russell left central Pennsylvania in 1825 with his young family, driving a team of oxen towards Buffalo. He ran the Cold Springs Tavern at what is now Main and Ferry Streets for a year, before buying the 200-acre Cotton estate. In 1841, he built the area's first brick home, a home which still stands today at 2540 Main Street (seen below in the 1880s).

Now painted white, the building houses "The Church in Buffalo," marked today by a sign proclaiming "Taste and See!" on the Main Street lawn. But for years, it was the McKendry-Dengler then Roberts-Dengler Funeral Home. It remains the oldest home still standing in Parkside.

Washington Adams Russell died in the home in 1877, but his name lived on famously in Parkside. Russell's son Washington Russell II went to California during the Gold Rush of 1849. His grandson, Washington Russell III was another prominent figure in local history, famous as an eccentric renaissance man.

Aside from having built the oldest building still in Parkside, the eldest Russell is also remembered as having been the source of four street names in Parkside. Deeded to the city in 1889, Russell Avenue was the cow path by which the family brought their cattle to drink from a spring in the Delaware Park meadow. Fairfield and Greenfield were the names of pastures on the Russell farm, located about where those streets are today. Orchard Place was the site of the Russell fruit tree orchard.

Col. William Chapin and Elam Jewett

Col. William Whitney Chapin stayed on at his father Dr. Daniel Chapin's home on Main Street following the doctor's death in 1821. Over the years, William built out from the somewhat rustic frontier cabin his father called home, eventually enveloping it completely. In doing so, with an eye towards aesthetics, he'd built what was considered one of Buffalo's most beautiful mansions. Willowlawn, he named it, for the willow trees surrounding the home. It was from one of these trees that Daniel Chapin took clippings to plant on either side of the grave in the Park Meadow. It is also from this estate that Willow Lawn, the small street between Crescent Avenue and Main Street, takes its name. Before Willowlawn Avenue was deeded to the city in 1905, it was the site of an expansive garden just to the south of the home.

The Willowlawn Estate, as it appeared in 1901 after a great storm which toppled a willow on the front lawn. An apartment complex now stands at the site, at Main & Jewett.

Col. Chapin died in 1852. Eight years later, in 1864, Elam Jewett, the publisher of Buffalo newspaper *The Commercial Advertiser*, purchased the Willowlawn Estate. It was Jewett's wealth, philanthropy, and keen eye as a developer that would help change the serene Buffalo Plains and Flint Hill area into the Parkside known today.

Elam Jewett was raised on his father's farm in Vermont, and wrote for several newspapers in that state. He grew restless however, and looked to the western frontier, "where great opportunities awaited him." He purchased a newspaper, *The Buffalo Journal from* Judge Samuel Wilkeson in 1838, and merged it with the *Advertiser* the next year. Having become a prominent Buffalonian in his own right, Jewett became a close friend of another prominent Buffalonian-- Millard Fillmore. The two traveled in Europe together in 1856.

Jewett's name on the mast head of an 1852 Buffalo Journal newspaper.

Jewett had "retired" to Willow-lawn to live the life of a "gentle-man farmer" on the massive acreage, but he did have several publicly-minded plans for his sprawling property.

First, with the War of 1812 still fresh in the minds of Buffalo, Jewett wanted to build a proper stone memorial to the hundreds buried in what was essentially now his backyard by Dr. Chapin and Captain Cotton. The *Mound in The Meadow* didn't look much different than it did 40 years earlier when the 300 soldiers were buried the spring following that "dreadful contagion" in 1813. It remained marked only by the pair of willow trees planted by Dr. Chapin, though the saplings had grown to full mature trees marking either side of the ghoulish reminder of the area's war history.

But it was ultimately through Dr. Chapin's previously mentioned efforts to keep and enhance the area's natural beauty that Mr. Jewett's patriotic intentions to build the monument were frustrated. The city took that majestic part of Jewett's land, and added it to the land also purchased from the Granger family, to make up the bulk of what is now Delaware Park. The mass grave remains to this day, underneath the Delaware Park Golf course, marked only by a large boulder placed by the Historical Society in 1896.

The wealthy publishing magnate also planned to give to his church in his retirement. Though his various plans were frustrated and also met with stops and starts through the years, Jewett eventually created a church that became the center from which the Parkside neighborhood would be built.

A devout Episcopalian, Jewett was rebuffed when he offered land to the Episcopal Church charity foundation to build a home and chapel for infants and the elderly on his land off of Main Street. Ellen Parisi talks about it in her book *A Century in the Fold: A History of the Church of the Good Shepherd* (1988), in part quoting Rev. Thomas Berry. Keep in mind, the *outlying area* referred to here is today the corner of Jewett Parkway and Summit Avenue:

> *It was felt unwise to leave the elderly and orphans stranded "miles from civilization" when the snowdrifts in winter would make walking anywhere impossible. "Here, the citizen dwelling below Ferry St. came out for a 'day in the country'... and here along the 'Main Street' the Williamsville stage rumbled in its daily trips to and from Buffalo. We were missionaries in those days, and tried to convince city merchants, who objected to delivering goods 'so far out,' that it as no farther out than it was in to make our purchases."*

This 1872 map shows Elam Jewett's vast property holdings, on both sides of the park, and both sides of Main Street.

But while Jewett's overtures were being rejected by his church because of the area's remoteness; it was just that feeling of "miles from civilization" that some in the bustling city were trying to capture. In 1858, the City of Buffalo was growing to a point where it looked like green space and nature was soon to be at premium. A group of "public-spirited gentleman" began plans to build a public park system in Buffalo. At private expense, Frederick Law Olmsted, the celebrated architect of the Central Park system in New York, was brought to Buffalo to "examine the situation and recommend a desirable park scheme."

Chapter 4: First a Park, then a Parkside.

Even as late as 1880, the area to soon be known as Parkside was still chiefly farm land, but an eye toward development had been sharply trained on the area for decades. Though most of the building in the neighborhood wasn't to be completed until the first two decades of the 20th century; it was the last two decades of the 19th century when the area began to take on a look familiar to what we know today.

First concocted in 1858, The Civil War interrupted plans for Buffalo's park system. It was 1869 when construction began of the masterpiece that would ultimately feature *The Meadow* at *The Park* (today Delaware Park) as its crown jewel. But even after the initial decade-long delay, the plan was an evolving one, even as shovels hit dirt.

As the park was being built, the city continued to grow. Olmsted changed the design of what is now Delaware Park as the outline of the Beltline Railway became apparent. In 1874, Elam Jewett built, paved, and maintained Jewett Parkway himself, as an easy entrance to the park for those getting off the New York Central Beltline railway. Other than Main Street, Jewett Parkway was the first street laid out in modern Parkside. Included in Olmsted's plans was a neighborhood he called "The Parkside," built around Delaware Park and Jewett's curving Parkway. It was first written of by Buffalo officials in the 1872 Parks report, in reference to *"The Park."* It's also among the first times the name by which a future community would be known was published.

An 1883 Olmsted map, including the Parkside Development. Note the different street pattern, with only one street where Crescent, Summit, and Woodard were eventually laid.

> *The Park, 3 and a half miles north of the City Hall, a ground designed to be resorted to solely for quiet rural enjoyment. The more notable features are, a grand sweep of undulating turf, one hundred and fifty acres in extent, and containing a goodly number of large well-grown trees, a body of water of forty-six acres, an open grove suited to picnics, and closer woods offering wilder and more secluded rambles. The Parkside, a detached suburb adjoining the Park on the north and on the east, designed by private enterprise, so as to secure to it a permanent sylvan character distinct from the formal rectangular streets of the city proper.... "Parkside," a district nearly three square miles in area, extensively planted, and guarded against any approach to dense building.*

Buffalo's Parkside was one of Olmsted's first attempts in his pioneering work in suburban residential planning, preceded only by his plans for Riverside, Illinois, a planned Chicago suburb. He laid out the streets in a gently curving, or curvilinear, pattern, encouraging leisurely travel. At the same time, the plan discouraged use of the neighborhood as a thoroughfare, with none of the streets leading directing to the city. Olmsted envisioned tree lined streets with boughs joining to create a canopy over the roadways. Parkside was meant almost as an extension of the park, serving to buffer his crown jewel from the bustle of Main Street and from future incongruous development, but also with an eye towards creating the ideal residential environment.

In 1871, a pair of young deer was donated to the Parks Commission by prominent Buffalo furrier Jacob Bergtold. A Deer Paddock was fenced in on the meadow, and the deer were put in the care of Elam Jewett. From this simple gift would

Animals were much more free range at the earliest beginnings of the zoo (above), but the modern zoo took shape quickly (below.)

grow the earliest origins of the Zoo, still operating on the same spot as that

original 1871 Deer Paddock. A pair of bison and 8 elk were added to the animal collection in 1895, and a zoo curator was hired the same year.

Two years later, the bear pits, designed to look like Roman ruins, were built as the zoo we now know was beginning to take shape.

In a cry that rings familiar in today's age, the 1881 Annual Report of the Parks Commissioner calls for ways to lessen the expense of maintaining the grass in the Meadow. What might be unfamiliar, though, is the method:

> *To maintain a trim and becoming appearance of the ground, frequent*
> *cutting of the grass in necessary... On the open areas, and more especially n*
> *the large meadow, much of the annual expense and waste of mowing might*
> *be avoided by pasturing. The meadow would maintain a large flock of sheep,*
> *which would by their presence, add much to the interest and naturalness of*
> *this part of the park.*

Sheep grazing in the Delaware Park Meadow, near Ring Rd. Aside from the sheep, only veterans of the Civil War on the civil service list were eligible to work in the parks.

For decades, sheep were seen grazing in the meadow in Delaware Park. Their presence on the broad lawn gave "an additional attraction to Park visitors, and served to give a natural animation to the quiet character of this portion of the park." Another quaint description from the Superintendent's 1886 report describes riding on the Meadow:

> *The meadow is open to equestrians whenever the turf is firm, but in the*
> *spring and late in autumn it is usually too soft. In a wet season like the last*
> *some portions are in an unfit condition about half the time all through the*
> *summer. Shutting off the equestrians from the meadow on this account*
> *causes perpetual friction, as the cause for such restriction is rarely*
> *understood, and an open stretch of smooth turf offers the best possible*
> *conditions for a free gallop. No method of constructing or maintaining a*
> *bridle road will provide so good a footing for the horse, or be so easy for the*
> *rider. But whenever the ground is wet, deep footprints are cut into the sod*
> *in galloping over it, and when these become dry and hard, horses are liable*

to stumble on them or sprain their joints. To enjoy permanently the privilege of galloping at full speed with perfect safety over the Park Meadow it is necessary that it should not be damaged by use when the ground is soft. Though few equestrians have appreciated this necessity, the risk of damage to the turf is so great that, so far as I am aware, no riding whatever is allowed on the grass in any other park in the country.

Horseback riding was soon joined by golf in the meadow; the course was laid out in 1886, nine holes were added in 1894. Bicycle riding was also a great fad near the turn of the century, and practiced often on the road around the meadow. The continued growth of the zoo also made the meadow area more and more popular with not just sportsmen, but families and those looking to take in the sunshine and fresh air.

In 1900, on the eve of the Pan-American Exposition, Frank Goodyear offered the city one million dollars to expand and beautify the zoo. Though this offer was rejected for political reasons, Goodyear's gift of Frank the Elephant was accepted, and the excitement surrounding the possibility of the large monetary gift emboldened planners and curators. The number of animals swelled to over 600. At the turn of the century, between 20,000 and 30,000 people visited the zoo and picnicked in the park each week.

Frank the Elephant spent his first few years at the zoo chained to a tree, before funds were raised to build a proper elephant house.

Right in the middle of Parkside, Camp Jewett was a tent city set up as inexpensive lodging for attendees of the Pan American Exposition in 1901. The rent was $1.50 a day for one of the tents, and one could take the "Main Street-Pan American-Zoo" trolley line directly to the Expo. Over 175 tents were set up on the entire block between Parkside and Woodward, and West Oakwood Place and Florence Avenue. The photo has Woodward in the foreground, and one can clearly see the Electric Tower (which stood at approximately Lincoln Parkway and Amherst Street) over the meadow. From the Collection of Len Mattie.

While planners continued to add features to make the park more accessible and more desirable to the residents of the nearby city, one feature that would make the park-- and the entire park system-- more sylvan and park-like was already there, ready to reap.

Just *Parkside* is a very apt name for the neighborhood as it stands today; its one-time appellation *Flint Hill* is just as likely, as any Parkside Gardener will tell you. The stone that gardeners find in their soil, is the same that was blown through to create the Kensington Expressway, the same that most Parkside basements are made from, and the same that was quarried just of Parkside Avenue near Florence Avenue behind the Olmsted Park's Lodge.

Onondaga Limestone is that ubiquitous gray stone embedded with chunks of black chert, or *flint*. "Black Rock" was so named because of the large outcrop of Onondaga Limestone, loaded with chert, that stuck out into the Niagara River near where the Peace Bridge now stands. The apparently useless Onondaga Limestone bridges behind the Delaware Park Lodge, on the golf course, once spanned the great hole made by the excavation of rock there.

The quarry was an early important element in the development of the park. Stone extracted from the quarry formed an early foot bridge over Scajaquada Creek, went into the construction of the state asylum, built the now demolished Farmstead (which stood where the Zoo parking lot is today), and built the bear dens and other rock formations at the zoo. The foundation of Buffalo's Parkway system was also made from crushed stone from the Parkside Quarry.

The Farmstead stood in what is now the zoo's parking lot from 1875-1950. It was the home and office of the Park Superintendent, and was built from limestone quarried from the park.

The last stone was mined from the site in 1897, but the old park quarry was transformed into a beautiful garden. When the Parkside Lodge was built in 1912, rustic bridges were built to span the chasm to link the lodge and bowling greens with the meadow. The current stone bridges, now at ground level, were built to connect the edges of the great hole in 1920.

The spot became the place where the young romantics of the neighborhood would take their love to see it blossom. In 1908, in a day before road and automobile safety standards we have today, the *Buffalo Express* reported that a couple died when their car plunged over the poorly marked edge of the quarry on a dark Saturday night.

The Quarry was a pit filled with gardens, behind the Parkside Lodge. The seemingly useless bridges there today once spanned the chasm.

Some of Parkside's earliest neighborhood activism and some of the earliest references to the neighbors of the park as "Parksiders" come in the form of rallying against proposed changes to the quarry. As Parks planners developed plans for a sunken gardens on the site, they also proposed building the park's stables there as well. Though Parkside was still early in its development as a residential community, the few that were here let their voices be heard against the building of the stables. An October 21, 1908 *Buffalo Express* headline blared, "Parksiders Make Good."

The following was written in the inimitable style of the turn of the century *Buffalo Express*, after the decision was made to place the stables in their current location, between Agassiz Place and Forest Lawn Cemetery, on the south side of what is now the Scajaquada Expressway.

> *For just about three hours after the decision was made, the park commissioners rested in the belief that all was satisfactory. Then they were undeceived. There was an uproar in the Parkside district which reached even to the respective homes of several park commissioners. And the howl was against the building of the new stable in the stone quarry, abandoned as that place might be.*
>
> *No, indeed, the stone quarry might be a bit wild. It might be the catchtrap for the flotsam and jetsam of the park system, utterly neglected and almost abandoned, yet the Parksiders did not deem it low enough to warrant its association with a stable. Petitions were circulated, public meetings held, persons who never before made public speeches made them, and the upshot*

of the whole matter was that the park commissioners decided they would build the stable elsewhere.

This 1908 victory would be the first of many for the ebullient residents who live between the Park and Main Street; Humboldt Parkway and the Beltline.

Lawn Bowlers on the court adjacent to the Parkside Lodge, 1912

Developing Olmsted's Parkside

Residential Development would come as to Parkside as it became easier to access. Main Street was paved in the 1830s, but it wasn't until the extension of street car service from Cold Spring to the Park in 1879, and the completion of the New York Central Beltline Railway in 1883 that living in Parkside was really made a viable option for many. Before those tracks were laid, the only two options for getting to the area were walking or taking a carriage. The Beltline tracks made a 15 mile loop around the city, and Buffalonians could ride from one end of the city to the other in about forty-five minutes, costing only a nickel. The train stopped twice in Parkside: The Highland Station was at Greenfield (near Jewett) and Main, and the Bennett Station at Amherst Street and Starin Avenue, where the station house and watchman's tower remain as private residences.

Elam Jewett and Washington Russell III sold portions of their property to the city in 1870 for Delaware Park, adding to the Granger acreage already set aside for the park. Russell, the grandson of the man who settled along Main Street in 1826, built himself one of the first homes of the

"Parkside" era on Main Street, in the shadow of his family homestead in 1885. Russell the Third was a lawyer, minister, mathematician, and musician who squandered much of his family's fortune on living the good life of a gentleman.

He built a Victorian showcase (seen above left), replete with the genteel finery of the era: A well stocked library, a music room, and a scientific laboratory. Russell III died in 1944, but his sister Lillian stayed on in the family homestead (above right) until the late 1960s. According to provisions in the family will, the 1841 brick home of Washington Russell was to be razed. Though the building had fallen into utter disrepair (right), after years of wrangling, the area's oldest home was saved, having served, as previously mentioned, as funeral parlor, and now a church. The Victorian home built by Russell III also survives on Main Street immediately to the south of the homestead.

Another early "Parkside" home belonged to the nephew (cousin by some accounts) of Elam Jewett, William Phelps Northrup. In 1870, he built a grand Victorian home on the southwest corner of Crescent Avenue and Jewett Parkway. The home adjoined the Jewett Family Willowlawn Estate just to the east.

The William Phelps Northrup Home, demolished 1950s. Currently, the Girl Scouts Building site.

While having an Uncle as one of the city's most successful printers couldn't hurt, Northrup became a success in his own right as a publisher of maps. His home was torn down in the 1950s, to make way for a Latter Day Saints Church (which still stands today as the Girl Scout Headquarters.) Northrup's barns, however, still stand -- today a private home-- set back from the street, immediately south of the Girl Scouts building on Crescent Avenue.

Even after handing over massive acreage to the city for the park, both Russell and Jewett still had large tracts of land between the Park and Main Street, land that was included in Olmsted's plans as "the Parkside." The initial plan for Parkside was bounded by Main Street, Parkside Avenue, The Belt Line Railway, Colvin Avenue, and Humboldt Parkway to the south. Olmsted's original vision called for Parkside as the ideal suburb: The curvilinear, crescent-like street patterns and lots as large as 100x100. If Olmsted had his way, the entire neighborhood would have looked much the way Jewett Parkway does today; large homes on large lots.

The problem was, in the beginning, people just weren't buying. The Parkside Land Improvement Company was formed in 1885, but development was initially slow. Olmsted was actually hired back by developers; retained to redesign the street layouts to allow for smaller lots, with Jewett Parkway remaining as the anchor and ideal showplace for the neighborhood. For the streets radiating from Jewett, the same basic design and intent was left intact, with curving streets and buildings set back, but less green space around each building because of the smaller plots.

Parkside Avenue, Crescent Avenue, and Greenfield Street were graded and surveyed with the smaller lots in mind in 1888, Woodward Avenue (originally *Davis* after an early Parkside Land Improvement Company investor) and Summit Avenue the next year. An 1892 ad from the *Buffalo Express* encouraged Buffalonians to come to Parkside:

Jewett Estate Lands- Beautiful Residential Section-- This area's many amenities include sewer, water, gas, new electric street cars, convenience to Belt Line, desirable lots, liberal terms for those wishing to build. Numerous advantages to the area! Giving you all of the needed rapid transit desires!

Of all those amenities, the fact that electric streetcars made their way to a still largely undeveloped neighborhood was likely most important. In a pre-automobile society, it was a major milestone in the further development of the neighborhood.

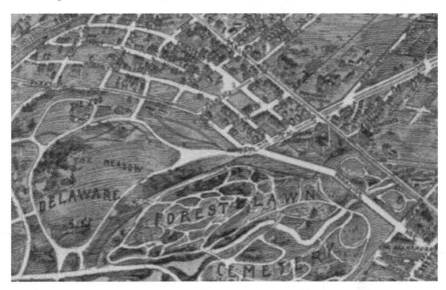

Can you spot the error? In 1893, a bill made it to the State Assembly with aim of extending Parkside at Agassiz Circle, straight through where Medaille College now stands, through the cemetery, straight through to Delevan Ave. That was rejected on the grounds that cemetery had already sold some plots in that right away, and the cost to the Buffalo Cemetery Ass'n would be too great. The makers of this 1902 map mistakenly showed Parkside running to Delevan.

Early Catholic Neighbors: St Vincent's and The Sisters of St. Joseph

While most of the earliest development inside what we know now as Parkside was an effort of mostly wealthy Protestant men, the Main Street corridor leading into the neighborhood was developed in large measure by the Roman Catholic Church.

St. Vincent de Paul church was built in 1864 on Main Street just south of what is now the Kensington Expressway interchange. St Vincent's

Roman Catholic Church was founded by the Rev. Joseph Sorg to serve the German-speaking Catholics who lived in the area. Generations of southern

Parksiders attended mass at the church just south of Humboldt Parkway on Main Street until the parish closed in 1993. When St. Mark's parish was established in 1908, the boundary line was drawn between the two parishes at Jewett Parkway, but was later moved south the West Oakwood Place.

The church grew fast enough that 3 different buildings, all on the same block, served as St. Vincent de Paul Church, each building growing larger.

Above: The original 1864 church, just before it was torn down in 1899. Below: Church and School, 1904

The most recent church buildings, built in 1924 in the Byzantine Romanesque style (see photo next page), are now a part of the Canisius College campus, and the church itself is known as the Montante Center. Many affluent Parksiders gave heartily to have the building erected.

St Vincent De Paul Church, Main and Eastwood, c.1926. After the church was closed by the Catholic Diocese, in the 1990s, the building was purchased by Canisius College and renovated as the Montante Cultural Center.

One of the Parkside area's earliest enthusiasts was Mother Mary Anne Burke of the Catholic Sisters of St. Joseph. Mother Mary Anne and her sisters marveled as they strolled up Main Street "north of the horse-drawn trolley tracks."

The Sisters of St. Joseph built a convent for novices, a novitiate, south from St. Vincent's to Delevan Avenue. The now densely built up property was then described as an "expanse of land and... groves of trees." A decade later, when the Sisters of St Joseph abandoned the property for the current site of St Mary's School for the Deaf, Jesuit Fathers purchased the land to farm in 1874. In 1911, the Fathers built Canisius College there.

The Sisters also purchased 30 acres of land across Main Street from St. Vincent's in 1883. The frontage of this land is now part of the Canisius College Campus, and the rear portion is Medaille College; Mount St Joseph Academy when it was built. Sister Mary of the Sacred Heart Dunne wrote about in *The Congregation of St. Joseph of Buffalo*:

No more desirable property than this, for its purpose, could be wished for. Situated at the north entrance to Delaware Park, overlooking the great expanse of Park Meadows and, on two sides, adjoining Forest Lawn, Buffalo's City of the Dead, the chance for seclusion was ideal. The place had been the home of George Bailey, an English Gentleman whose artistic taste led him to lavish time, care, and wealth upon a spot already beautiful by nature. It was known for many years as one of the finest estates in the surrounding country with its extensive lawns, patterned garden plots, fruit orchards, patches of forest with trees from every clime and a charming residence of English Architecture. Time brought about a change of fortune for the owner and there was a rumor of putting the property in the market for sale. Many who had hoped one day to secure it were deterred from opening negotiations because of the price when a fire occurred. The residence was destroyed and a sale became imperative. The fact that the pastor of the nearby church saved the life of the owner, now an invalid, by carrying him out of the burning structure, dispelled whatever of prejudice may have existed against letting the property fall into Catholic hands.

That was the sanitized version approved for publishing in the Sister's official history. The well told tale told by early Parksiders was closer to what Michael Riester wrote in the *Parkside News* in 1998:

For years, Mother Mary Anne Burke had pleaded with Bailey to sell the former S. V. Ryan estate to the sisters. Despite his refusals, Mother Mary Anne prayed that he might change his mind. By 1883, Mr. Bailey was elderly and an invalid when Rev. Martin Phillips, Pastor at St. Vincent's, was aroused from his slumber by the roar of fire at the Bailey Estate, directly across Main from the church. Father Phillips risked his own life, charged into the building, and saved Mr. Bailey. Soon thereafter, Bailey sold to Mother Mary Anne and the Sisters of St. Joseph, who erected a motherhouse on the grounds in 1889.

The Mother-house, Main Street, 1899.

The cornerstone laid in 1889, the Mother House and Academy of Mt. St. Joseph was completed on the site of the former George Bailey home by 1891 for the sum of $80,000. From the 80 foot vantage-point of the cupola, it was written that "the panorama of the entire city was visible, and, on clear days, the shining mist of the mighty Niagara (could also be seen)."

Mt St Joseph Academy, Main at Humboldt, 1891

To raise money to add to the buildings the Sisters had constructed, in 1908, the Sisters sold ten lots facing Humboldt Parkway and raised $150,000. Coming full circle, these properties, and the homes on them are now the property of Medaille College, which was originally built to house Mt. St. Joseph School for Boys.

Mother Mary Anne was a forced to be reckoned with, but also a gentle soul. On the Anniversary of her silver anniversary as a sister, Fr. Patrick Cronin wrote in the *Union and Times*, on December 26, 1888, "A woman of rare worth is Mother Mary Anne. Large-minded, just, generous and kind, her heart and brain have especially fitted her to be the guide of

St. Mary's School for the Deaf, 1898.

others... The history of her life and labors would be the History of the Sisters of St. Joseph in western New York. The tiny mustard seed of three Sisters and four deaf pupils in 1854 has developed into a body of one hundred-fifty Sisters, fifteen schools, a property unequalled for beauty... and an Institution for the Deaf which is the rival of any other of its kind."

Anna Bancroft Coushaine wrote about the *St. Mary Le Couteulx Deaf Mute Institute* in the Buffalo Courier in 1901, saying it had been furnished with "every modern convenience to be had in the home of wealth and refinement," and was a great atmosphere to for the pupils to learn to "talk with their fingers, which they do just as rapidly as hearing children can speak with their lips."

The Church of the Good Shepherd

Back in the middle of Parkside proper, in the mid 1880's, Elam Jewett began plans for developing a piece of his property to act as a central meeting place for the fledgling Parkside neighborhood, to honor his friend and late pastor, and to serve as a beautiful place of worship.

As previously mentioned, Jewett was a devout Episcopalian, and was a vestryman at Trinity Episcopal Church downtown. He and his wife were rather close with the pastor of Trinity, Rev. Edward Ingersoll. When Ingersoll died in 1883, Jewett made every attempt to join with the church in an attempt to build a suitable memorial to Ingersoll. When an agreement on what was to be done couldn't be reached, an aged Jewett poured all of his energy into an effort that would memorialize his friend, and at the same time cut down his long, dusty ride to church every week. Plans for the Ingersoll Memorial Chapel, soon to become Good Shepherd Church, were set in motion.

The Church of the Good Shepherd, 1890

From his time at Trinity, he was acquainted with men and women of the relatively new and idealistic Arts and Crafts movement. He contacted the firm of Silsbee and Marling (later Marling and Burdett) to design the church. Herbert Burdett was an early assistant in the office of H.H. Richardson, and helped capture the *Richarsonian* style that Jewett was after in his church. Work began in 1888, with the cornerstone laid just months after Elam Jewett's death in 1887.

As the structure was being completed, it was outfitted with nine prime examples of Louis Comfort Tiffany windows, most notable the representation of the Good Shepherd carrying two lambs in the chancel. The work was said to be among the last works to be done by Tiffany himself.

Another Tiffany window, a scene of Christ with children, is found in Good Shepherd's children's chapel. The children are said to be modeled after the children of Jewett's nephew William Northrup, as well as other kids of the neighborhood. *(See above.)*

As published in *A Century in the Fold: A History of the Church of the Good Shepherd,* Good Shepherd's first pastor, Rev. Thomas Berry, wrote his view from the back porch at Jewett's *Willowlawn* estate, as the church was being built. Parkside was still rather rural in 1888:

> Contiguous to the lawn yet separated from it by a picket fence and a hedge of stately roses, was a garden. Oh! What a garden with its old fashioned flowers and its prim borders, where children romped and through which Mrs. Jewett often led her guests. Departures from the house were always accompanied by gifts of flowers or fruit, wile the tables of many less fortunate people were literally kept supplied with vegetables in season.

The first service was held at Good Shepherd in March 1888, at which time from the steps of the brand new church, the Rev. Berry could see only trees, grass, and the Jewett Homestead. It was Jewett farmland for as far as the eye could see, and it was from that corner that Parkside was to blossom.

Only two years after that first service at Good Shepherd, in 1890, prominent Buffalo Architect William Sydney Wicks, partner of E.B. Green in the firm Green and Wicks, built his English Tudor mansion across the street from Good Shepherd on the corner of Summit Avenue and Jewett Parkway. Wicks was an early and long time promoter of the Parkside neighborhood, and kept his neighborhood in mind as served as Park Commissioner from 1897-1900. The Wicks Mansion remains to this day one of the more recognizable landmarks in Parkside.

William Sydney Wicks, c.1896, in front of his home on Jewett, with Good Shepherd in the background.

Darwin Martin

In 1902, the corner of Summit Avenue and Jewett Parkway saw construction begin on what was to become Parkside's most famous landmark, as the complex of buildings designed by Frank Lloyd Wright for his great patron Darwin Martin began to rise from the earth.

A prominent figure in the organization of the 1901 Pan American

Exposition in Buffalo, and eventually tabbed by President Wilson for a National Defense post during the First World War, Darwin Martin moved to Parkside in 1897. He built his first house about a block north of the home now known as the "Darwin Martin House," at 151 Summit Avenue.

An executive at the nationally popular and successful Larkin Soap Company, Martin was a millionaire by the turn of the century, and decided to build a home commensurate with his family's lifestyle and their place in Buffalo Society. Having come from a broken home and spending his youth working in a host of odd jobs, Martin also hoped to provide room on his new sprawling estate for his extended family, including his brothers and sisters.

After flying to Chicago to meet with the young Frank Lloyd Wright, Martin commissioned him to build his sister a home. The Barton House, built for Martin's sister Delta, and her husband, George Barton, was the first of several buildings erected on the Martin Complex in 1902. She was the only Martin sibling to take him up on his offer of a home in Parkside.

An early view of the Darwin Martin house, from before 1911.

By 1906, the main house-- The Darwin Martin House-- was ready for move-in by the family. It's low, horizontal-lined Prairie style design was (and is) certainly a contrast with the more traditional home styles in the neighborhood.

The complex, complete with the main home, the Barton House, a Gardener's Cottage, a carriage house, a pergola, a conservatory, a stable, and a porte-cochere, was Wright's most expansive prairie style project, and one of the largest home complexes he ever built. The home's "Tree of Life" windows are instantly recognizable the world 'round.

While many scholars have often looked to the architectural masterpiece as Wright's finest example in the Prairie style, the biggest endorsement came from Wright himself. Plans for the Martin House long hung in on his office wall, described by the architect as "a well-nigh perfect composition."

Wright also designed a home for another Larkin Executive in Parkside. In 1908, the Walter V. Davidson home was built at 57 Tillinghast Place. Martin would also have Wright design his lakeshore summer home, Graycliff, in Derby, in 1927. It was also

Davidson House, 2000. Greg Lodinsky photo

almost entirely on Martin's word that Wright was retained to build the Larkin Headquarters on Seneca Street. The pioneering office building was torn down in 1950. Eventually, over a lifetime of patronage, Martin was either directly or indirectly responsible for the commission of at least 15 Wright buildings. When Darwin Martin lay dying in 1935, Wright wrote to Martin's wife Isabel that their friendship was a "blessed relationship to treasure and travel on."

Chapter 5: The Growth of Parkside

Buffalo's population doubled in size between 1890 and 1930, and one of the city's hottest new neighborhoods was there to help absorb the growth. Around the turn of the century, a Parkside address became very desirable, and unlike other parts of the city where a single developer or builder put up an entire neighborhood, in Parkside, each individual land owner hired their own architect and builder, creating the architecturally varied place that still makes Parkside unique.

Above :23 Agassiz, Home of John Eckert

Below: 415 Crescent, Home of Edwin Sutton

Prominent architects like Stanford White, Esenwein & Johnson, Max Beirel and E.B. Green built many houses to impress throughout the neighborhood, many with third floor or basement quarters for servants. When built, the neighborhood attracted many prominent Buffalonians. Names familiar generations later, like Mathias Hens and Patrick Kelly. Yes, Hens and Kelly lived on Summit and Crescent respectively, where their backyards touched. While many generations of Buffalonians associate 998 Broadway with the name *Sattlers*, Mr. Sattler made his home in Parkside, as did William Simon of the Simon Pure

Above: 438 Summit. Below: 82 W.Oakwood

Brewing Company. The Mayor of Buffalo and founder of the Holling Press, Thomas Holling, also lived in Parkside at One Agassiz Circle.

But for all the amazing architecture and wealthy citizens Parkside attracted, the neighborhood also welcomed those of a more middle class means. School teachers, plant workers, and food brokers made their homes in Parkside as well as lumber and machining magnates. A stroll through the community is a primer in fifty years worth of popular residential, church, and commercial architecture. From late Victorian and Queen Anne, down the line to Shingle, Bungalow, Prairie, Romanesque Revival, Colonial Revival,

Tudor Revival, right up to the venerable and well represented American Four-Square; all are on display in the living museum that is the neighborhood.

With people and their homes, came the supporting businesses and organizations to the neighborhood to service the new community. It was a transition from outlying outpost to hot-to-trot city neighborhood, and it was a change at least one Parksider watched from beginning to almost present day.

Bob Venneman was born in 1912 on Amherst Street in a house built by his father. A long time friend of Parkside, Venneman died in 1998, and his lifetime of memories provide a singular view of the change the

neighborhood has seen. He spoke of his memories of the tavern and stage coach near East Oakwood on Main, with a blacksmith shop close by, and the handful of businesses in the three story red brick building that stood where the Amherst Street Metro Rail station now stands. In a 1988 interview with the *Parkside News,* Venneman talked about the chestnut trees that grew between the houses and sidewalks all up and down Main, and the elms between the sidewalks and the streets. He said many of the trees didn't make it when Main was widened in 1931. Growing up, he said, the Parkside neighborhood looked very much

Above, right: Parker's Hall, East Oakwood & Main. Above: Central Park Market, site currently Amherst St MetroRail station

the same as today. North of Hertel, though, he remembers there being practically nothing.

Venneman also remembered walking past the original Park School, which was on the "Willowlawn" property on Main Street between Willowlawn and Jewett Parkway, before it was developed for the housing that is currently on the block. "It was a fresh air school, composed of five or six shelters, only one of which had heat. In the winter, children sat at their desks wearing a garment similar to a sleeping bag. They learned to print using mittens. They went a bit over-board on the fresh air." The school moved to the corner in 1913, but had moved to Snyder by 1920. Shortly thereafter, the homes currently on the block were erected.

A few blocks away, meanwhile, another private school was moving to Parkside; this one a fixture in the neighborhood to this day. Nichols has been a Parkside neighbor for a century.

Nichols School, Amherst St. near Colvin c. 1930

An account of the day says "Several Buffalo men joined forces to buy the Glenny property at Amherst Street and Colvin Avenue; an ideal locality for a school of the kind is the wooded land lying north of the park and Amherst Street." The Nichols School was named for its first headmaster, William Nichols, who began the school in 1892. He had died the year before buildings on the present campus opened in 1909.

Parkside Business

Parkside had a different feel during this simpler time. There wasn't a street in the neighborhood without a business of some sort. In many homes, the front parlor served as an office for doctors, dentists, and lawyers, and as a workshop for dressmakers, tailors and even a furrier. And that was just the businesses in the homes of the professionals. The Main Street ends of both West Oakwood Place and Greenfield Streets were dotted with businesses.

On the first block of West Oakwood Place, in 1940, there was a grocer, Beatrice Foley selling gifts, Frank Nashek selling furs, a dry cleaning company, and the Jean Alma Beauty Shop. In 1950, Greenfield Street had Joe Mobilia's shoe repair shop, Abe Kramer the tailor, George Meyer's grocery, Frances Wolkiewicz's variety store and Klein's Delicatessen.

In 1930, 11 Greenfield Street was home to Flickinger's; one of the original small shops that would grow later into the Super Duper chain. Flickinger also ran a grocery store at Parkside and Russell, a corner that through much of the neighborhood's history has also been a traditional business strip. In 1930, there were 4 stores listed as grocers near Parkside and Russell.

As Burt Flickinger and family were looking at their Parkside businesses and thinking bigger, one longtime Russell Avenue grocery was thinking on a small scale; a small scale that would serve it well as a Parkside institution for 50 years.

From 1924 to 1976, the Flett Brothers, Jack and Wally, were literally at the beck and call of Parksiders and North Buffalonians for their grocery needs. While a shopper could walk into the store to shop, it was one special service that the Flett's kept up long past any of their competitors that kept customers coming.

Long into the era of chain grocery stores, like those pioneered by their one time neighbor Burt Flickinger, Flett's delivered on orders their customers phoned into the store, usually on old fashioned tab credit. Jack would fill the orders as they came in, and Wally would drive the delivery truck, carrying your groceries to your front door, and even your kitchen table.

The store was in the second building in from Parkside on Russell Ave, next door to the Park Meadow. Wally's daughter, Ann Marie, fondly remembers her dad at the store. "He could hold beans in his hand, and tell you when there was a pound. They had fresh fruit and vegetables, and canned goods, and they had the butcher shop. Once the supermarkets started coming in, it was just the delivery service that kept them going, because they could just pickup the phone and have their groceries delivered. There were a lot of wealthy customers who didn't mind paying a little more to have their groceries delivered."

Ironically, the site of the current grocer on Parkside, wasn't the site of one of the dozen or so grocers in the neighborhood over the years. Before Wilson Farms stood on Parkside, the lot was the home of a Hygrade (and later Gulf) filling station and garage from the 1920s until 1976, when the current building was erected. It's

Wally and Jack Flett, inside their store, after it was announced they'd close in 1976. Wally drove the delivery truck, and Jack would put the orders together called in by servants or the women of the various homes not only around Parkside, but all over the city, and as far away as Williamsville in later years when Flett's was the last grocer to still deliver their goods.

fondly remembered by generations of Parkside kids as *the* place to fill up bicycle tires at the *always free* air pump.

While many kids made their first dimes working at the area grocery stores, a very young Bob Venneman worked at a different Parkside landmark. He was a stock boy at the Fairfield Library, at Fairfield and Amherst Streets. On payday Friday, he'd go to Unterecker's (later *The Stuffed Mushroom*, then Shawn B's, at Main Street and Orchard Place) for a 15 cent ice cream sundae. He quit that job with the depression hit and his pay was cut back to 19 cents.

The Fairfield Library, opened in 1925, and shutdown by the Buffalo and Erie County Library in 2005, was designed by Parkside resident William

Sydney Wicks. Originally Parkside Unitarian Church when the doors opened in 1897, the building is considered one of the area's finest examples of New England Colonial architecture. In 1912, the building became the home of the

Parkside Evangelical Lutheran Church. A dozen years later, in 1924, the building was purchased by the city and opened as a library in 1925. The

The Fairfield Library, c. 1930

building was enlarged in 1961 to accommodate more books, but the Fairfield Library was closed but the Buffalo and Erie County Library in 2005 in the midst of an Erie County budget crisis. When built, it was one of many churches to be built in the Parkside neighborhood as the community grew.

The church was built by the man greatly responsible for developing Parkside's neighbor to the north; north of the Beltline tracks, that is. There lies the Lewis J. Bennett-designed and developed neighborhood *Central Park*. The owner of Buffalo Cement began planning the neighborhood in 1889, taking four years and $300,000 to lay out streets, plant 1200 elm trees, blast out bedrock, and built the four stone markers to delineate the original boundaries of this exclusive neighborhood. Strict zoning ordinances set forth by Bennett called for homes of at least 2 stories, with barns in the rear of all residences. Specific price structures were also established, with homes on Depew to cost a minimum of $4000, on Main Street $3500,

Bennett himself had a magnificent 24 room home (right) built at 354 Depew, which was later razed and replaced by 12 lots.

and on Starin, $2500.

A vice-president of Pierce-Arrow, Mr. Henry May, lived at 290 Depew Avenue. Many Parksiders and Central Park residents became used to Mr. May driving through the streets of the neighborhood on a drivable chassis without a body, working out the kinks in the latest Pierce-Arrow models before they went to production.

The train station at Starin and Amherst belonged to the Buffalo Cement Company and was leased out to the New York Central Railroad. Once the Beltline discontinued service in the 20's, the station was sold to the Boy Scouts and used as the headquarters for Troop 12 until well after World War II. The structure remains the last standing station house that served the Beltline railway.

Indirectly, Bennett also played a role in the development of Parkside, but mostly by his unwillingness to accept a Roman Catholic church into the community he was developing.

In 1908, Buffalo's Catholic Bishop, Charles Colton, wrote of his desire to start a new parish in "the Central Park area of Buffalo," either to be called Epiphany, or St. Mark's. Bennett had reserved triangular islands of land throughout Central Park, upon which churches were meant to be built. Parkside Lutheran, for example, is one those "churches on an island," where Depew Avenue, Wallace Avenue, and Linden Avenue all meet.

The people of St. Mark and the Buffalo Catholic Diocese inquired about one such island, at Beard, Starin, and Morris. Developer Bennett, whose own strong Unitarian views were greatly at odds with Catholicism, refused to allow a Catholic church on his property, or anywhere in his Central Park development.

Fearing similar responses to overtures across Amherst Street in the Parkside Neighborhood, the founders of St. Mark's went cloak and dagger, and perhaps by stretching the truth in a few places, were able to buy several lots only two blocks away from that initially desired triangular lot, this one at Woodward Avenue and Amherst Street.

A very young priest, Fr. John McMahon, was offered the chance to become pastor of the parish. His background as pastor at Mt. Carmel Church would serve him well. Mt. Carmel was down near the Commercial Slip in Buffalo's *rough and tumble* waterfront /canal district, right next to where the

St. Mark's first church, a small wooden structure, was constructed in the summer of 1908, where St Mark's School now stands. More specifically, the church was where a hedge now stands in front the school on Woodward, parallel to the northernmost wall of the school building. The building to the left predated the church, but is currently serves as the rectory, enclosed in the same stone as the church.

Crystal Beach boat would dock. The area, known as "The Hooks" in those times, was filled with interesting characters from many different walks of life, while Parkside and Central Park were still greatly undeveloped. It was many of these *rough and tumble* sorts who made up the 30 or 40 families who started St. Mark's. The families were mostly those of men who were dockworkers at the commercial slip at the canal terminal. There were also 70 or 80 servants, virtually all Irish, among the congregation. They were the maids and butlers in the larger Parkside and later Central Park homes.

St. Mark was a mostly Irish parish, which differentiated it from the other close by parishes like the former St Vincent De Paul (the building is now *The Montante Center* on the Canisius College Campus) and Blessed Trinity Church (on Leroy Street) which were mostly German parishes. The new parish began June 25, 1908.

Almost immediately, parishioners started raising money for a permanent church. In 1914, ground was broken; work was completed the next year. The statuary near the altar of the current church-- likenesses of

Jesus, Mary, Joseph and Anthony-- were the only artifacts that made their way from the original church to the current building. It was at this time that the rectory, a wooden frame Parkside Home that predates St Mark's, had a stone facade built up, to give it the same look as the church.

St. Mark was different from other new parishes of the time, in that the parishioners built a stand alone church first without a school. Many new parishes of the time, like North Buffalo neighbors St Margaret's and Holy Spirit, built combination church/schools, with the church on one floor, the school on another. Parishioners settled on waiting a few years for a school, which was built in 1920-21, and still stands today. That first pastor, Father McMahon, would spend 20 years at St Marks, until he was named the Bishop of Trenton, NJ in 1928.

Presbyterians also have a long history in Parkside. A long time neighbor at Main Street and Jewett Parkway, Central Presbyterian Church was founded in 1835 by a group of 29 folks looking for a more conservative theology than that which was being presented at the more liberal "new school" First Presbyterian. They organized as Pearl Street Presbyterian, and their first church was a large log cabin just north of Genesee Street. Under the 38 year leadership of their first pastor, The Rev. D. John C. Lord, the church remained the only "old school" church in the area. A new church was built in 1837, then another in 1852, at the corner of Genesee and Pearl Streets, on the site of the current Hyatt Hotel.

While by 1900 the membership had grown to over 600, the quick turnover of several ministers, and a 1906 fire at the Pearl Street home of Central Presbyterian Church left the congregation with a rapidly dwindling number, and in some financial difficulty.

Park Presbyterian Church was organized in Parkside in 1893, and worshipped at Parker's Hall at Main and Oakwood Streets (see photo on page 51). A small church was built on Elam Place in 1897 (currently the home of Refreshing Springs Church, see 1909 photo, above.). In 1909, the congregants at Central and Park voted to merge. The Pearl Street building owned by Central was sold to the Shea Amusement Company, and by 1911, the combined church, under the name Central Presbyterian, began worship in a new church at the corner of Main Street and Jewett Parkway(currently Mt. St. Joseph's Academy). In 1914, the church had a membership of 688, but over the ensuing 12 years, "enjoyed a phenomenal growth which is without parallel in the history of (the) denomination."

The explosive growth was almost immediate. By 1926, only 14 years later, the numbers had swollen to an amazing 3,378. The relatively new building had to be enlarged to fit the larger flock. The almost inconceivable plan to do so was so incredible, that the producers of MovieTone News shot the feat to be included in news reels all around the country. The stone facade of the church was moved 40 feet closer to Main Street, all in one piece.

Central Presbyterian Church (now Mt.St. Joseph Academy) Main &Jewett, 1930s

A new pastor, The Rev. Dr. Robert MacAlpine, and his charming personality were largely responsible for the growth. MacAlpine had radio broadcast equipment installed in the church at a time when the medium was still a novelty, sending his voice and message near and far to those listening on "wireless sets" all over Western New York, inspiring them to come to Sunday Services at Central Pres. Ten stained glass windows were added in 1940, in 1957, the school building was added behind the church.

Chapter 6: Getting Around Parkside and Beyond

The Beltline Railway, which helped open up Parkside to

development, was eventually too industrial for the sensitivities of the upwardly mobile new residents of Parkside to handle. One of life-long Parkside resident Bob Venneman's earliest memories was of a 1918 freight train crash. He spoke of the crash with the *Parkside News* in 1988.

> *The trains met head-on on a curve opposite the Amherst Station. Dad and Mother walked me up there. All the trees were singed for a long time. Of course, all the tracks were lowered 16 feet in 1909 when Lewis Bennett, the developer of Central Park, objected to the noise of the trains. Wooden stairways led down to the tracks.*

That, however, is only part of the story. In the spring 2005 edition of the *Parkside News*, Michael Riester tells the story of the Beltline tracks having once been embedded in Parkside Avenue—right at grade level crossing Parkside-- where the viaduct between Crescent and Linden is now *(Above, with street car, 1940s)*. The story of why that intersection was dug out, and why the viaduct is now there, is a grisly one.

> *On October 15, 1897, the Scatcherd Daughters, Emily and Dorothy, and their aunt, Miss Emily Wood, were returning from a visit at the William Ball residence at the corner of Depew and Starin Avenues.... The story goes; the carriage driven by Miss Wood proceeded toward Parkside Avenue, where they intended to enter the park. Because of gale force winds that day, the carriage was tightly secured; the side curtains drawn. Mr. Ball noticed a west bound train coming from Main Street, and noticed that because of the wind, the warning whistles were muted, almost negligible. Sensing disaster, Mr. Ball ran after the carriage as it sped towards the Parkside crossing; however, before he could make it, the engine of the train slammed into the carriage containing the two girls and their aunt. With tremendous force, amid the terrible screeching of brakes, the train pushed the carriage*

and its occupants as far as the Colvin Crossing, where it finally came to a halt. The horrified engineer enlisted the help of the groundskeeper at the nearby Glenny Mansion (now the site of the Nichols Athletic Fields) to recover the lifeless body of little 11 year-old Dorothy. The mangled bodies of her sister Emily and her aunt were rushed to Buffalo General Hospital at the order of Dr. Bainbridge Folwell, who happened to be visiting Mr. Glenny. Miss Emily, age 5, died shortly after being removed from the carriage. Miss Emily Wood was pronounced dead by Dr. Roswell Park.

The father of the little girls, John Scatcherd was to become known as "The Father of the Grade Crossing Commission," and fought to have grade level tracks eliminated on a city- and state-wide basis. He lived to see the excavation of the road and erection of the Parkside viaduct in 1911, followed shortly thereafter by the elevated bridge at Colvin Avenue. The trains of the Beltline were powerful. One of the engines regularly used along the tracks that surrounded Buffalo was Old' 999. On a New York Central run between Syracuse and Buffalo in 1893, with Engineer Charles Hogan at the throttle, the 999 set the world speed mark. Its 112.5 miles an hour was the fastest that man had ever traveled up to that point.

New York Central Engines like this one carried the Beltline passenger cars roaring through Parkside from the 1870s through the 1950s.

While the Beltline was removed from the road, the IRC Trolley was still sharing the roads with horses, carriages, and the occasional automobile. Trolley service started in Parkside when only a few houses dotted the landscape in 1898. The was known through the years as the Kenmore line,

IRC Streetcar at Parkside and Jewett; fence is gone, but the corner post remains in front of the Zoo parking lot. 1940s.

the Parkside line, and the Zoo line. By 1911, residents were suing the IRC to get better service to the area. Portions of the lawsuit, as published in State Public Service Commission Documents, are worth including here not only because they show the growth of Parkside, but are also very descriptive of what the area looked like in 1911.

> *The principal complaint is centered in the irregularity of the service, its insufficiency, and the crowded condition of the cars. The lines complained of leave the Terrace in the city of Buffalo, proceed northerly about 4 1/2 miles upon Main street, turn westerly at Florence avenue to Parkside, to Hertel, through Hertel to Virgil, to Kenmore, and (outbound) to Tonawanda. The service particularly criticized by complainants is that given to residents of that portion of the seventeenth ward through which the lines pass: that is, between the turn off at Main street and Florence avenue and the turn off from Hertel to Virgil. The territory here situated is in a growing part of the city, and it was shown that a number of residences have recently been built in that section. ... The territory between the corner of Hertel and Parkside eastward to Main street is well built up in the eastern portion, and several houses have recently been added in the western portion, but it can not be called compactly built territory. On the north side of Hertel avenue there is a long stretch of vacant land practically covering the entire distance from Main street to Parkside avenue. Parkside avenue at its northern end is also very sparsely built up. The residents of this section in going to the business*

portions of the city must either use the Kenmore-Zoo cars or the Main Street cars. The Main Street service is frequent, and it became evident on the first hearing that if better facilities were furnished to the residents of this portion of the city to get to Main street a considerable number would avail themselves of that method of downtown travel.

Even as the automobile began to grab a foothold as a means of transportation, the trolley remained an important means of moving around the city. Ann Marie Flett, the daughter the grocer Wally, grew up on Russell in the 1940s.

My grandmother used to take my brother Bill and I on the street car downtown. Every Saturday we'd take the trolley to Laube's Old Spain for lunch, and we'd go to the show to see a movie. Around Christmas time, Mother would take us on the street car down to AM&A's to see the windows, and all those people downtown. It was always nice.

I loved the street cars. It wobbled back and forth, especially when you crossed onto another street. It went up Parkside, then Florence, then up Main Street downtown, and there was always alot of clickety-clack when it went onto Main Street because there were so many tracks on Main. The cars were well-swept, but a little worn-down. We mostly took the Main cars, but there were street cars on Hertel and Delaware, too.

Streetcar trips by Parkside kids weren't always adult supervised adventures, though. Tom Malamas, whose family owned The Parkside Candy Shoppe, can recall being one of the many of the youngsters of Parkside scrapping together the few cents necessary to hop on the street car to find out what fun could be had elsewhere in the city. "You could catch the trolley at Parkside and Oakwood, or at Main and Oakwood in front of the Candy Shoppe. I loved those big street cars, but it sure was a wobbly ride."

The Kenmore/Zoo/Parkside trolley line was abandoned, and buses began following the route in June, 1950. Trolley service stopped in the city on July 1, 1950, replaced by motor busses.

The late Al Kerr spent a lifetime photographing trains, streetcars, and anything having to do with traction, including many of the photos on these pages. Little did he know, that his photographs would serve, decades later, as one of the best glimpses into everyday life in Western New York in the 1940s and 50s. His son, Fred Kerr, said traction was always his dad's passion.

Parkside at Jewett, 1940s, Al Kerr photo

"He was a train buff, and this all started at a very early age. He lived and grew up in the Kensington area, and he was friends with many train enthusiasts. It became his passion, too. He became involved in the National Railway Historical Society, over which he was a member for over 50 years. He loved railroading, but his passion was traction, and that meant street cars. He traveled all over the United States, collecting timetables, and photographing trains and street cars. Of course he took a great number of photos in the Buffalo/Niagara Falls area."

Parkside near Florence, 1946

Photo by Al Kerr

"When you have a passion, just like someone who runs marathons, or loves ships, or aviation, it was his hobby. He loved street cars, interurban lines. He loved steam engines, he loved riding trains; he traveled all around North America on trains. He never flew in his life. He loved doing it, he loved giving speeches about trains and street cars. The library at the NHRS Museum in Tonawanda is called the Albert D. Kerr Library."

Above: From Parkside onto Hertel.

Below: South on Parkside from Linden

When trolley/street car lines were extended past Delevan Avenue towards the city line starting in the 1880's, Main Street became a clickety-clacking spaghetti-style stretch of interweaving city lines, until the last street cars were removed from service in 1950. 30 years later, mass transit moved under Main Street, and several neighborhood landmarks made way for *MetroRail* Stations.

One of two houses removed to make way for the *MetroRail* Humboldt Station, The Frank-Culliton House was an unassuming brick home built circa 1865-1875, and at the time of its demolition in the 1980s was one of the oldest in the area. Mr. Frank's son was an architect, and designed the neighboring apartment building, which was built to serve visitors to the Pan American Exposition in 1901. The Culliton family bought the home in 1911, moving to Buffalo from Niagara Falls. Culliton was in the stone business,

Though still an oft traveled intersection for Parksiders, it would take a well-trained eye to identify the corner of Main and Humboldt. It was taken before the expressways were blasted through the area, and before the LBJ Apartment complex was built. The brick Frank-Culliton House stands where the Humboldt station now stands.

and dredged the track bed for the Beltline Railway, as well as numerous homes and businesses, like the Sears Store at Main and Jefferson (later Blue Cross, now the Canisius Science building), and the Ford Factory (now the Tri-Main Building.) Mike Riester wrote of the house at the time the wrecking ball swung in 1985. "The home's stately mid-nineteenth century exterior of neat red brick quietly reminded those who passed by of the graciousness of an earlier age, when Main Street was both rural and residential."

Just as Parkside rattled 70 years before with the blasting out of the Beltline railbed, January, 1982 had the north end of Parkside shaking for track-laying once again for the Amherst Street *MetroRail* station. At the time, officials projected that it will be the second busiest stop along the *Metro*Rail route, with 9,700 passengers arriving and departing each day. Only the Lafayette Square Station was expected to be busier. While in 2008 the NFTA had no way to quantify the numbers arriving and departing at each stop, spokesman Douglas Hartmeyer says there are approximately 23,000 passengers on the entire *Metro Rail* system each day.

"The Main Street"

Of course, following the rail and the streetcar to Parkside soon enough was the automobile. *King's Official Route Book* was the *Mapquest.com* of the early automobile era. It gave new drivers not only street names as far as getting from one place to another, but offered landmarks as well in an era when street signs may not have been the most reliable or varied. In the 1913 edition, the book makes notes of several landmarks you'd see driving on Main Street from downtown through Parkside on your way from Buffalo to Batavia.

Buffalo, N. Y., to Batavia, N. Y.,
38.6 miles, Road mostly all brick and state road.
0 Leave Soldiers' Monument and Park on right, go north on Main St., following trolley .
0.7 Pass Teck Theater Bldg. on left
2.3 Intersection of trolleys with car barns on right (Cold Springs Street Car Barn)
2.6 Passing hospital on right (Sisters Hospital at original Main/Delevan location)
2.7 and Forest Lawn Cemetery on left
2.8 Pass Carnival Court Park on right (amusement park where Main and Jefferson meet)
3.0 St Vincent of Paul's Church on right (now Canisius College

Montante Cultural Center)

3.1 Mount St. Joseph Academy on left (now Canisius' Lyons Hall)

3.3 Providence Retreat on right   (current site of Sisters Hospital)

3.4 U. S. Marine Hospital on right   (currently Benedict House)

3.5 Deaf Mute Institution on right, straight ahead through

3.6 Parkside brick schoolhouse on left (in current School 54 parking lot)

3.8 Central Presbyterian Church on left   (now Mt St Joseph's Academy)

3.9 Cross cement bridge over R. R.

Between the businesses in the Parkside neighborhood itself, and the business along Main Street, it was possible, for much of the neighborhood's history, for someone living in the area to not have need to leave the neighborhood for months at a time.

Without Main Street, there would not have been a Flint Hill or a Parkside. While over the last two decades its become the re-invigorated Hertel and Delaware Avenues that are the local shopping and dining destinations for Parksiders, for the 200 years previous, it was Main Street that served most of the needs of the people of the area we now call Parkside.

Over a three year period, third generation Parkside Resident and Definitive Parkside Historian Michael Riester wrote a series of articles, published in the *Parkside News*, examining the history Parkside's portion of Main Street and role the stretch of road played in the life of the people of the area through the two centuries since the path was first carved from the wilderness.

> *(I)n 1850, the city secured vast tracts of Erastus Granger's farm on Flint Hill (as Parkside was then known.) This land, with its rolling hills, large open meadows, woods, and Scajaquada Creek was considered the most beautiful and scenic in the area. 80 Acres would become Forest Lawn Cemetery, but the land to the north and west of the then-proposed cemetery, including Granger's meadow and quarry, would be reserved for parkland. It would be some years yet before the landscape architect Frederick Law Olmsted would draw on its natural beauty to create Delaware Park. "*

> *By the 1880s, once "The Park" was developed, and the modern streets of Parkside were laid out, the character of Main Street changed dramatically. Large homes, like the brick Victorian of the Garris Family at Main and Robie were being erected. The Garris family made their fortune in the Jammerthal quarries near Grider and Kensington.*

Riester puts forth the thesis, "As goes Main Street, so goes Parkside." The following pages will take a look at Main Street in three separate sections: The institutions of the area, the automobile showrooms, and, finally the small businesses; the shops and storefronts where most people did most of their spending and buying of goods and services.

Main Street Institutions

Many modern Parksiders, who just think of the whole area as "Canisius College," will be surprised to know that the block of Main between Delevan and Jefferson has been home to a brewery, an amusement park, and for over 50 years, a Sears & Roebuck store.

While visible in this photo of the Schnaezlin Brewery snapped circa 1900; Today, Scajaquada Creek is underground from Forest Lawn Cemetery all the way to Cheektowaga. The photo is from behind, the bridge is part of Main Street.

In 1842, Jacob Schaenzlin moved into a brewery built two years earlier at 1857 Main Street, near Scajaquada Creek. This is the present site of the Delevan/Canisius *MetroRail* station.

Further up the block, and a half century later, at the point where Jefferson Avenue and Main Street meet, stood an amusement park, which was known by at least 3 different names over the decades it was open. First known in the 1890s as Athletic Park, its name was changed first to Carnival Court, then to Luna Park, when it was purchased by the father of the modern

Above: Looking north up Main from the From the Top of Chute the Chutes. That's Jefferson Avenue, St. Vincent's, then Providence Retreat (now Sisters Hospital)

Below: Buffalo Athletic Field Main Street Entrance (between Jefferson and Delevan)

amusement park, Frederick Ingersoll. He owned the park from 1904-1920. Among the more popular rides was the "Shoot the Chutes" water ride, which Ingersoll built in all his parks, and was the basis for the modern water flume ride.

The midway of the Carnival Court was heavily damaged by fire in 1909. The fire was briefly mentioned in the *New York Times*, calling the place a "pleasure resort," and mentioning the skating rink and the theatre suffered damage in the blaze.

Closed and abandoned by 1920, Sears and Roebuck purchased the property and built a store on the site in 1929. From that Sears store, generations of Parksiders were clothed, and kept in appliances, hardware, paint, and gardening supplies. Sears left in 1980, and four years later, the building became the headquarters for Blue Cross and Blue Shield of WNY. The building, which once housed all that the Sears Catalog had to offer, is now Canisius' Science Hall.

George Zornick lived on Russell in the 1960s. "Sears was very convenient to the neighborhood. As a kid, I remember the big escalator in the middle of the store. We'd go there for clothes and my dad for hardware; the place seemingly had everything.

The fate of the Main Street land immediately north of Jefferson Avenue was sealed when Jesuit Fathers purchased it, described as an "expanse of land and... groves of trees," as a farm from the Sisters of St. Joseph in 1874. In 1911, the Fathers built Canisius College there, and have been growing it, and buying more land and buildings to expand their campus, ever since.

Though now the gentrified, commanding presence along that portion of Main Street, Canisius College moved to the area at a time when Catholic institutions weren't necessarily welcomed with open arms in all sections of the city. This wasn't a problem on this stretch of Main, however, given the fact that the new school was flanked by a well-established Catholic church, Catholic hospitals, several Catholic elementary and high schools, and a convent.

The land was wilderness far beyond the edge of the city when St. Vincent de Paul Parish was founded in 1863. Bishop John Timon and Rev. Joseph Sorg established the church to serve the mostly German quarry men and farmers in the Kensington-Humboldt area. It was, according to the parish's 100th Anniversary History booklet, "a peaceful, wide open location removed from traffic and congestion of the city." As already discussed, three successively larger churches were built over 60 years. The first 1860's wooden church became the school when a larger brick church was built in 1887. And as the neighborhoods surrounding the church, including Parkside, grew, by 1924, the need developed for yet another, newer, larger church building. The Byzantine-Romanesque style, final home of St Vincent de Paul was opened Thanksgiving Day 1926, with over 5,000 people in attendance. When the church closed in 1993, Canisius College bought the buildings of its old neighbor, and renamed the exquisite Byzantine building the Montante Center.

Also as mentioned, the Sisters of St. Joseph were major developers of Main Street, having first strolled north of the horse-drawn trolley tracks

(which then ended at Delevan Avenue) to built their *novitiate*, south of the church, where Canisius College now stands, and moving the Deaf Mute Institute to the corner of Dewey and Main in 1898. The name was officially changed to St. Mary's School for the Deaf in 1936, and continues to be the longest continuously operated institution in the Parkside neighborhood.

Aside from teaching at both St Vincent's and St. Mark in Parkside, The Sisters also ran Mt. St. Joseph's Elementary and High Schools, founded in 1891. The high school was closed in the mid 1980s, but "Little Mount" survives to this day. The Sisters of St Joseph decided to close the school in 2005, but parents and alumni banded together to keep the school open. The school moved from a building recently torn down on the Canisius campus to the former Central Presbyterian Church complex in 2007.

Mt St Joseph (High) School For Boys, 1923. Now Medaille College.

In 1937, Mount St. Joseph's Teachers College received its charter from New York State to award degrees in Education. In 1968, the curriculum expanded, men were welcomed to the campus for the first time, and Medaille College was born.

Sisters of Charity

The Sisters of St. Joseph haven't been the only Catholic nuns along the Parkside section of Main Street. The Sisters of Charity established Buffalo's first hospital downtown in 1848, and moved to the corner of Main Street and Delevan Avenue (the current home of the Canisius College Koessler Athletic Center) in 1876.

And while *Sisters Hospital* didn't move there until the World War II era (1943), a hospital of sorts has stood on the spot where Sisters now stands since the Civil War era. The Providence Retreat, also known as through the years as the Providence Insane Asylum, and the Providence Lunatic Asylum, it was established in 1860 by Dr. Austin Flint and Dr. James Platt White, with the help of the Sisters of Charity.

As the Civil War dawned, after it was "decided that the city needed a hospital for the treatment of mental and nervous diseases." The institution opened its first building on the Main Street grounds July 15, 1861. That building was then outside the city limits, on grounds described as "spacious and beautiful." The grounds contained both a hennery for eggs and a dairy, and "stronger patients" were able to take advantage of the neighboring Delaware Park and Zoological gardens.

The Providence Asylum, 1870s. Sisters Hospital stands on this spot today.

The asylum, and its most infamous guest, nearly cost Buffalo a Presidency. One of Buffalo's most scandalous residents was a "guest" at the Providence Retreat. Maria Halpin was one of many unwed mothers residing there, and she became a star in the 1884 Presidential campaign. It just so happened that the prominent Buffalo attorney with whom she reportedly had a tryst quickly moved up the ranks as Mayor of Buffalo, then Governor of New York, and ultimately President of the United States.

Had Grover Cleveland run for President in this modern age, the intense vetting process likely would have knocked him out of the running early. The Halpin story was well-known but not talked about in Buffalo for at least a decade. However, when Grover Cleveland decided to run for the White House, *The Buffalo Evening Telegraph,* a paper similar in journalistic integrity to the *National Enquirer,* ran a story entitled *"A Terrible Tale-Dark Chapter in a Public Man's History."*

The rag put into print a damning piece of salacious bombast slanted against Cleveland by his old Western New York political enemies. The paper spelled out that Cleveland was the lover of *The Loose Widow Halpin*, and when she became pregnant, the powerful Cleveland had her institutionalized, the child placed in an orphanage, all at Cleveland's expense. The story spread like wildfire around the country, to the delight of Cleveland's political opponents.

A familiar song on the Presidential campaign in 1884 went, "Ma, Ma, where's my Pa? Gone to the White House, ha, ha, ha." Grover Cleveland paid for the institutionalization of his one-time lover-- the mother of what possibly was his love child-- at Providence Asylum, which stood where Sisters Hospital stands today.

Though painted in the worst possible light, Cleveland couldn't and wouldn't deny the story. Halpin actually kept the company of several prominent lawyers, many of them married, including Cleveland's partner and best friend Oscar Folsom. Folsom was nearly positive the child was his, but to save Folsom and the other men potential martial problems, the bachelor Cleveland took responsibility for the care of the woman and her child, whom she named Oscar Folsom Cleveland.

Cleveland asked a judge to commit Halpin to the bucolic Parkside mental ward only after he was unsuccessful in trying to break her of alcoholism. At Cleveland's expense, his young ward was place in the finest orphanage to move along his placement with and adoption by a well-to-do family.

These details, however, were only made public decades later. Despite the controversy, Cleveland was elected President, where he was the first man to be married in the White House. Not to Halpin, who continued to hound Cleveland for money, but to Frances Folsom. The daughter of his partner Oscar, Cleveland became her legal guardian when she was 11 years old. She was somewhat scandalously 27 years younger than the President, and, though it wasn't common knowledge at the time, was likely the half sister of Cleveland's "son." For his part, Oscar Folsom Cleveland eventually became a very successful doctor; his education paid for by the man who took a political hit for doing what he thought was the right thing.

A More Modern Hospital

As modern medicine progressed, particularly in the newly developing field of psychiatry, a new state of the art "Asylum" was built in

1905. Bishop Charles Colton was assisted by Msgr. Nelson Baker in laying the cornerstone for what was then known as *The Providence Retreat*. The building was to be fireproof, and "up to the high standards required by the state... in the treatment of the insane and feeble minded."

Bishop Colton and Father Baker assist in laying the cornerstone for the Providence Retreat, Main at Kensington & Humboldt. This building still stands; greatly modified and added to, as Sisters Hospital.

A 1905 *Buffalo Express* article notes, "The institution is managed by the sisters, under the rules approved by the state commission of lunacy." The article goes on to talk abut the $300,000 building. "Away in the back, and

distinct from the others, are the rooms for violent patients who may be noisy."

1905: Sisters of Charity as their new hospital is started. St. Mary's School for the Deaf is in the background.

In 1943, the 83 year old Providence Retreat, long the home "for treatment of mental patients," was closed and converted to a maternity hospital. Upon the opening of *Louise de Marillac* Hospital, an official told the *Buffalo Evening News*, "We feel there is more need here for an additional maternity hospital

and an enlarged institution for babies than for the care of the mentally afflicted that the Providence Retreat has been carrying on."

Three years later, ground was broken on another million dollar expansion of the structure that was destined to become the new Sisters Hospital at Main Street and Humboldt Parkway. The new streamlined, modern structure was prepared to combine

The Providence Retreat was not alone in catering to the psychological needs of Parksiders. Dr. S. A. Dunham was the superintendent of Parkside Sanitarium, 1392 Amherst Street. It was established in 1902, and had a capacity of 25.

the efforts of the *Louise de Marillac* Maternity Hospital and Sisters Hospital. The hospital was on *the cutting edge of modernity*, with a telephone and radio in every room.

Easily ignored, standing between Sisters Hospital and St Mary's School for the Deaf is a rather nondescript brick building with a lesser known rich history. Built in 1907-10 as the US Marine Hospital, it's likely to have gone unnoticed by most passersby for over a century. The building served as a home "owned and operated by the United States Government, and is for general medical service to sailors, marine soldiers, ex-soldiers, marines and merchant seamen" for almost 50 years. Far and away the most common, interwoven maladies amongst the old seadogs were old age and alcoholism.

US Marine Hospital; Main Street, between St. Mary's School for the Deaf and what is now Sisters Hospital. 1930's postcard.

In three separate incarnations, this building has played, and continues to play, a role in the forefront of medicine. First, as the Marine Hospital, many early strides in anesthesia were made inside the walls of the Parkside institution. Very early in his career, it was here that one of the world's pioneering anesthesiologists first learned his trade, at a time when the specialty at best was an after thought. In an Article in *Anesthesia and Analgesia* in 2000, Drs. Ronald Batt and Douglas Bacon write about Dr. Clarence Durshordwe, a World War I veteran who grew up on Buffalo's East Side and attended UB Medical School.

> *After medical school, Durshordwe interned at the 68-bed Marine Hospital in Buffalo. On completing his training, he was hired as an assistant surgeon*

for the Public Health Service. Early in his five years of service, he discovered
that the lowest ranking physician was assigned to give anesthetics.
Concerned that he might harm a patient, Durshordwe went to Buffalo City
Hospital to observe nurse anesthetists administer anesthetics. Toward the
end of his tenure at the Marine Hospital, now assigned to perform surgery,
Durshordwe found he spent more time worrying about the anesthetic than
the surgical procedure.

The greatly self-taught doctor would be one of the men who helped
bring together the theories and practice of anesthesia from locations all
around the world; where even late into the mid-20th century some
physicians around the world still questioned it's medical value.

Great strides were also made in the fledgling practice of physical
therapy when the federally owned hospital was transferred to the state in
1950, and it became the home of UB's Chronic Disease Institute. It was the
area's first hospital devoted to "physical medicine, the combination of
medicine and therapy." Within 3 years of the doors opening, the institute
"achieved remarkable results in restoring to partial or complete usefulness
disabled limbs, muscles, and organs, and overcoming speech difficulties." It
was here that many of the tenets of 21st century medicine were first explored
locally.

As of 1953, two years before the polio vaccine was announced to the
world, and at a time when the diagnosis meant fear, every polio patient
brought to the facility in an iron lung was able to gain release from the
"cumbersome contrivance." One arthritis patient, so seriously disabled he
was brought into the center on a stretcher, walked out, self-supporting, eight
months later; all by virtue on the modern medical theories we now take for
granted, first explored locally by our Parkside neighbors.

The Marine Hospital Campus was purchased by Sisters Hospital in
1995 for off-street parking for visitors and employees. While the original
plans called for the building to make way for even more parking space, *The
Parkside Community Association* advocated saving the historic structure. This
was accomplished when *Benedict House* was opened at the Main Street
location in 1997. It's mission, as taken from its website in 2008:

The mission of Benedict House is to provide non-discriminatory residential
housing opportunities and supportive services for persons living with AIDS
in an environment promoting the principles of dignity, respect,
understanding, compassion and self-determination.

Buffalo Public School 54

When the Jewett and Russell farms were opened for building sites about 1890, among the first questions was of adequate schooling for the children of families coming to live in this new part of town. Many schools in the surrounding areas were old and filled to capacity.

The year 1892 saw public education come to Parkside, when *"The Parkside School,"* a brick school house which was to eventually become School 54, was opened on land donated for the purpose by Mrs. Elam Jewett.

In marking the 35th anniversary of the school, a 1927 Buffalo Sunday Times Article, stated, "The history of School 54 runs parallel with the history of the neighborhood surrounding it." This brick building stood in the current school's parking lot.

Originally a 16 room school, the building grew as the neighborhood did; additions came in 1905 and 1913. The later addition was really more of an encapsulation, with the original facade being enveloped completely by the new build.

Part of what made the school an institution was the continuity of the teachers and staff. The school's first principal, Miss Clara Swartz, lived a few blocks away at 154 Woodward Avenue. Her tenure at the school ran from the school's opening until her retirement in 1924. Thirty years worth of Parkside youth all had the same principal at the Parkside School. Toward the end of Miss Swartz's tenure as principal, came Miss Mary Kirsch, who began teaching first graders in the early 1920s. She would teach generations of Parkside 6 year-olds before her retirement in the early 1960s.

While these two women, whose careers spanned 70 years in education, were both remembered for their warmth with the children, Miss Schwartz was also remembered for patrolling the halls with the rubber hose. She used it liberally on misbehaving children.

Part of School 54 Class of 1936, Main St in background.

The school has long had one of the strongest Parent-Teacher Associations in the city, as early as 1920, making sure that the school was always among the finest in Buffalo. The group often won the favor of city officials, winning upgrades for the school like a new cafeteria, more classrooms, and an improved heat plant.

As the years wore on, dress codes banned slacks for girls, and dungarees for everyone in the 1950s. The school day began with a morning prayer, and, even after Miss Schwartz hung up her hose, corporal punishment was still a means of making sure students fall into line.

But School 54 changed as Buffalo and Parkside did, and those changes, and how they were carried out, is a major part of Parkside's identity through the 60s, 70s, and 80s. More on that part of the story is yet to come.

One big change came in the mid-1960s when ground was broken on the current School 54. In 1964, the last vestige of Parkside's agrarian past was demolished; as Hagner's Dairy was taken down to make way for a *new state of the art* school building.

In the early days of the Delaware Park Zoo, the directors decided any animals that died would be donated to the Buffalo Society of the Natural Sciences. In 1895, when an American Bison died at the Buffalo Zoo, experts from the Smithsonian Institution said no one in Western New York had the skill to mount the animal. Herman Grieb's attempt was not only successful, but "Stuffy" the bison remains on display at the Buffalo Science Museum to this day. In 1915, Grieb moved his family and his taxidermy shop from Elm Street to the more rural block of Main Street between East Oakwood and Jewett. The building was next door to the Buttolph farmhouse, which was demolished in 1929 to make way for the Pierce Arrow Showroom. The Grieb Studio eventually made way for the adjoining lot.

As students past and present gathered to watch the demolition of the old school that so many had passed through, memories flowed of not only the school, but of old Main Street.

Marjorie Hagner, whose family home and dairy gave way for the new school, remembered when, the generation before, elegant residences of the Grieb and Berger families were leveled to open up space for the Cadillac and Oldsmobile dealers directly across the street, making car lots between the Tinney/Braun and Streng showrooms.

Buying a Car in Parkside

The Parkside area of Main Street became home to many upscale motor car showrooms. They included the Hupmobile Showroom (soon to be Dick Willats Hudson Dealership, photo on previous page) next to Smither's Parkside Pharmacy at Leroy Avenue, as well as the popular Studebaker showroom between East Oakwood and Dewey Avenues. One could also buy a Pierce-Arrow or even a venerable Ford in Parkside as well. The Ford

Factory and showroom was at the corner of Main Street and Rodney Avenue, along the northeast side of the Beltline tracks.

While the factory on the north side of the Beltline was turning out cars for working men and women of the country, both metaphorically and literally on the other side of the tracks was the "Update Building" for the ultra-elegant Pierce-Arrow. Built in Buffalo on Elmwood Avenue, The Pierce-Arrow motor car was the status-symbol car of choice for John D. Rockefeller, Babe Ruth, Presidents Taft, Wilson, Harding, and for dozens of Hollywood stars, like Carol Lombard. The siren girlfriend (and later wife) of Clark Gable, Lombard purchased a Pierce-Arrow in 1926. Later, the company began to offer hydraulic brakes. Never wanting a starlet to be without, the company paid to have the auto shipped back to Buffalo by train, unloaded off the Beltline into the Update Center, new brakes were installed and the car shipped back all at Pierce-Arrow expense. It was typical for Pierce-Arrow owners to ship their cars to Parkside for yearly maintenance and updating.

The update building remains, but for most, Pierce-Arrow in Parkside means the showroom. In 1929, the showroom moved from Main Street between Tupper and Edward to the Main Street at Jewett Parkway location, which until that time was the site of Floss's Coal and Ice. The $500,000 masterpiece building, along with the Central Terminal and City Hall, is one of a handful of fine Buffalo buildings built in the style that would become known as "Art Deco." Crowned by a 40 foot tower, the building's exterior boasts windows friezed with polychromed terra cotta. Inside, the coffered ceiling is adorned with tire and hub medallions. The floor could accommodate up to 15 luxury automobiles.

One Parksider, Milt Carlin, then a teenager, remembers when the Shah of Persia's Pierce Arrow was featured the showroom window along Main Street. Milt recalls the thrill of being one of many neighborhood kids who tagged along with the crowd invited to view the elegant black car with its opulent jeweled ashtrays and white bear rugs.

While in 1929 there were 1,500 Pierce-Arrows motoring around Buffalo, the timing for the move to the brand new, state of the art showroom couldn't have been worse. The nation would soon be in the grips of an economic depression. Sales dropped off, and by 1936, the Pierce-Arrow showroom had become a Cadillac showroom. Cadilliacs would be sold from the spot for the next 62 years under 3 different names. First Maxson Cadillac from 1936-57, then Tinney Cadillac from 1957-81. Finally, from 1981-98, the dealership was known as Braun Cadillac. When Braun moved its showroom to Depew, Buffalo Savings Bank purchased and renovated the space as their headquarters branch. In 2007, Buffalo Savings was bought out by First Niagara Bank, which continues to run a branch at the Jewett & Main location.

Just to the south of the Pierce-Arrow showroom, stood Eagan & Streng Chrysler starting in 1923. The building of green marble became an Oldsmobile dealer in 1930, and when Eagan died in 1938, Herbert H. Streng's name went up on the sign alone. The Streng family spent 75 years selling cars in Parkside at 2365 Main Street.

In 1973, the Strengs bought the property between their dealership and Tinney Cadillac to the north, adding room for another 60 Oldsmobiles, making the dealership the largest in WNY.

Only weeks after Braun Cadillac closed in 1998, Herbert S. Streng, the son of the founder of Streng Olds announced General Motors bought the dealership back from him, effectively ending the ability of Parksiders to buy a new car in the neighborhood. "I just sold one customer his 30th Streng Olds. GM isn't just buying a dealership from me," Streng said upon news of the closure, "They're buying a lifetime."

Canisius College bought the Streng Dealership building, and in 2001 opened Demerly Hall there. The green facaded building now houses the school's health and human performance graduate programs.

In the 1940s, Saul's Auto Sales was a Studebaker Showroom across from West Oakwood, and Don Allen Chevrolet was at Main and Fillmore.

Next door to City Chevrolet was the Central Park Theatre, right at the point of Main and Fillmore. Long time resident Marjorie Hagner remembered it as a true neighborhood movie house, with the latest great moving picture shows, along with vaudeville acts. Ads from the 1946 City Directory.

But Parkside's first foray into the world of the automobile came decades before Streng or Pierce-Arrow. The Ford Motor Company opened their sales, service, and assembly operations plant in 1915. It was designed by Albert Kahn and Ernest Wilby, who based the building on that of an earlier Ford plant in Cambridge, Massachusetts. You can still see "FORD" inlayed in the brick on the smoke stack of the building as of 2009. The showroom was on the ground floor, manufacturing on the higher floors.

From 1915 to 1923, 599,232 Model T Fords were assembled at the Main Street facility. The last Model T rolled off the assembly line in Buffalo in 1927. Then from March 1928 to August 1931, Model A Fords were built in Parkside until all Ford's local manufacturing was transferred to the Fuhrmann Boulevard/Woodlawn plant.

After Ford moved its machinery from that building to a plant of Fuhrmann Boulevard in 1931, Bell Aircraft took over the plant through 1942. During that time, Bell produced the Airacomet P-59, America's first twin-engine jet warplane. Initially called the XP-59A (right), and disguised with propellers on the jet engines, the plane never saw wartime service, but did provide the ground work for the US's venture into the jet age. In May 1942, the CNX Corporation, a subsidiary of the Hercules Motor Corporation,

churned out diesel engines for the US Navy, and did so through the end of the war. More to come on the war effort in Parkside.

 Once the war was over, in 1945, Trico Products Company bought the structure and manufactured windshield wiper components at the building from the early 1950s through 1987 at what was known to Trico workers at Plant 2. The old Ford plant became the multi-use Tri-Main Center in 1988, and continues to serve both sides of Main Street with dozens of offices, studios, light industrial plants, and shops of many different sizes.

Much sprang up around the tracks laid down along, over and under Main Street. In 1905, The Highland Masonic Temple was built by architect EB Green; predating the Central Presbyterian Church and Presbytery Buildings next door to the south. The lodge got its name from the Highland Station, the Beltline stop directly across Main Street, to the south of the tracks.

Once train travel gave way to the automobile, the Highland Station was torn down in favor of a gas station. This photo dates from the 1940s, and clearly shows the Ford/Trico Plant as the backdrop. With the gas station torn down, in 1987 Broad Elm started construction on the site at the corner of Main and Jewett. In 2005, The Montante Family donated the plot of land to the north of the tire shop to the community as "The People's Park." It's cared for and maintained by the communities surrounding it on both sides of Main Street.

The Backbone of Main Street

Gert and Ernie Schmitter were just two of dozens and dozens of small business owners who have made a living and a life along Main Street. And while the institutions written about thus far gave gravitas and stability to the area, it was the smaller mom and pop shops, where people did their day-to-day consuming, that are remembered so richly and warmly by the people who called Parkside home during Main Street's heyday.

Schmitter's Card Shop was a long-time tenant of the triangular building that stood where the Main/Amherst MetroRail Station stands today. Carl Schmitter photo.
(see the building on p.51)

The corner of West Oakwood Place and Main Street was the heart of the business district that served Parkside, and at the heart of that corner: One of the most warmly remembered shops to ever grace the Parkside section: Parkside Candy Shoppe.

The shop delighted young and old alike at the corner of Main and West Oakwood for generations. First opened by the Kaiser Family on St. Patrick's Day, 1917, the Malamas Family took over the operation in 1944. Tom Malamas spent a great deal of his young life at the soda fountain then owned by his parents and his uncle.

"You walked in to two long cases of candy, we had 14 booths, and 6 stools at the soda fountain." During that time, the noon time luncheon menu was very popular, as was ice cream in the evenings. The exterior and the soda fountain were featured in the 1983 film "The Natural," and Malamas says the scene was very reminiscent of what it was actually like inside Parkside Candy Shoppe in the 40s. "People would come from all over for our hot fudge sauce and chocolate syrup. I was too young then to think of it, but I wish I had those recipes now!"

But it wasn't just the candy and ice cream. Ted and Sandy Malamas were lauded when they finally closed up the store in September 1986, after over 40 years of operation. "They had strong religious and civic pride that made them an integral part of the Parkside neighborhood. They weren't just selling ice cream and candy, they were selling quality and devotion."

From the front door of Parkside Candy, one could see car dealerships, including the Studebaker shop across the street car tracks, Central Park Bowling Lanes, the druggist, the hardware store, a delicatessen, a grocer...

Historian Mike Riester has done the counting: In 1915, three bakeries, several meat, poultry, and green grocers, a tailor, toy store, a bowling alley, barbers, dentists, a hardware store, dress and hat shops, and the Kaiser Candy Company (to become Parkside Candies in 1930) were all several steps from Main Street and Oakwood Place.

Riester says without a doubt, the golden era of business along the Parkside section of the main thoroughfare was in the late 1920s and 1930s.... An incomplete list of businesses includes; Hawser's Bakery, Clock's Bakery, Red & White, Stokes Candies, Carillon's Jewelers, Thomas Taylor Shop, Russell's Barbershop, Ruchte's Hardware, Wangler, Marion's Ice Cream, Rychert's Florist, Bald's meats, and the Bills' Sisters Delicatessen at East Oakwood, which featured Stellar's Almond Rings.

Santora's was Parkside's First Pizzeria at 2500 Main Street, and was the location from which all of today's incarnations of Santora's sprang. Directly across Main from the Ford/Trico/TriMain building, it has served over the years as an American Legion Hall, a dance studio, and the United Auto Workers Union Hall. Since 1994, it has been the site of Buffalo OB/GYN Womens Services, and is often surrounded by protestors as one of the regions last remaining abortion providers. Slain Doctor Barnett Slepian practiced there until he was shot and killed in his Amherst home by anti-abortion extremist James Kopp in 1999.

But it was places like Parkside Candies-- places where a kid could satisfy a sweet tooth that seem to be remembered better than most. Unterecker's served ice cream and candy near at the corner of Main Street and Orchard Place in the 1920s, and two Parkside Drug stores had complete soda fountains, Dwyer's and Smither's.

DWYER'S PHARMACY
ROCCO BALLACCHINO, PROP.

2248 Main St. corner Florence

Buffalo, New York

Telephone: 834 - 1649

WE ACCEPT MEDICAID PRESCRIPTIONS

SMITHER & HILL
DRUG CO., Inc.
Phone 833-1111

2339 Main St
Corner Le Roy
Buffalo, N. Y

SMITHER'S
RELIABLE PHARMACIES

"If it's a prescription take it to Smither's"

These ads appeared in a 1967 St. Mark's bulletin.

Dwyer's, later Woldman's, was on the corner of Main Street and Florence Avenue, and retained the feel of an 1800's apothecary up until it closed in the 1970s. Aside from the soda fountain, Dwyer's is remembered by many for the rainbow sherbet cones served there.

Robert Knight Smither opened the "Parkside Pharmacy" in the 1880s at the corner of Main Street and Leroy Avenue. There it, too, remained until the late 1970s. Many generations of Parkside residents got their first job at Smither's, where Karl Smither and Don Hill were the bosses.

Longtime resident Jack Anthony's father owned a drug store at Fillmore and Rodney, but also has fond memories of Smither's. "Merle Alderdise... he grew up on Greenfield... and I would skip out of services at *Central Pres* when the minister would start his sermon, and we'd go up to Smither's at Main and Leroy, and eat a sundae, and get back before anyone noticed."

But inside those dozens and hundreds of shops, were the shopkeepers. Real characters that helped make more interesting in an earlier time. When the following article on "Frank The Barber" was written for the *Parkside News* in 1981, he had seen virtually all the history talked about in this Main Street chapter unfold outside his shop window, in the section of store fronts just north of Central Presbyterian Church and the Highland Masonic Lodge, and to the south of Greenfield Street.

Almost 50 years have passed since Frank the Barber came to Parkside to cut hair. Today, (April 1981) the oldest active businessman in our neighborhood, Frank Notaro, 77 years young, doesn't even seem ready to quit! His shop, located on Main Street just north of Jewett, has served generations of families, including some notable residents of our city...

Frank can go on and on telling of the many customers and their sons and grandsons and even great-grandsons who he was served. The shop, which opened in the 30's, makes you think of days gone by. The 1938 Zenith Floor Model radio is still used everyday. "I had the first TV in the area for a barber shop," Frank adds. The comic books and magazines bring back many memories of the past. The shop has a delightful glow of nostalgia.

Frank came to America in 1912, from Alimunusa, a small town in Sicily. He began a shop across Main Street in 1932, and moved to the present site in 1940..." He and his wife Genevieve were married and have enjoyed 53 years together. The Notaros are residents of Parkside and have raised two daughters. Pictures of his son-in-law and grandson in the service hang on the walls of the shop. He was quite a bowler in his day, participating in leagues at St. Marks and Central Presbyterian Churches. The Notaros attend St. Mark's Church.

Frank and Genevieve Notaro have made Parkside their home and work. Their beautiful Christmas window display, featuring ceramic and china figurines, is enjoyed by all who pass by during the season. The Notaros have never returned to Frank's homeland. Parkside has always been their home.

Frank Notaro retired in 1983, and took a piece of Parkside Americana with him. Al Villa was another longtime businessman. His *Buffalo Lawnmower Service and Sales* business was on Main Street, just north of West Oakwood Place, from 1963 to 2005. Al once shared with me his secret to good health: Chocolate milk. For years, Al says he'd get it ice cold right off the milkman's truck, and it's good for anything from headaches to upset stomachs.

Just as it is today, but even more so in the past, one couldn't walk too far along Main Street without running into a doctor's office or an undertaker. One doctor, a dentist, in fact, had his office next door to Al Villa's shop.

The offices of Dr. Monreith Hollway, were also at various times a Barber shop and a jewelry store. Obscured by the tree in Buffalo Lawnmower, where Al Villa sold and repaired lawnmowers for over 40 years. 1970s photo

Dr. Monreith Hollway retired in the 1970s, leaving the storefront (above) mostly vacant for nearly 2 decades, until March 1987 when the Parkside Community Association began the process of acquiring grants to buy and renovate the property for the group's offices, and low income housing in the one-time dentist's office upstairs.

Of course, there were places for adults to congregate *as adults* as well. Once prohibition was lifted, there were two long-time popular taverns. Grabenstatter's, near Dewey Avenue, and Diebold's red brick tavern, at the corner of Leroy Avenue, both serving to quench the thirst of Parksiders, and the German immigrants on the east side of Main Street. Grabenstatter's Restaurant became Margaret Kaufmann's Copper Kettle. One of Parkside's first Main Street businesses, in the days of the stage coach to and from Williamsville, was a gin mill.

John R. Schardt, Jr. ran a tavern at 2095 Main Street (near Kensington), and was doing so in 1911. By 1915, the saloon's liquor license was in the name of John J. Brinkworth, whose descendants ran the Park Meadow Bar and Grill at Parkside and Russell, as well as numerous other taverns and businesses around the city up to this day. The building was vacant by 1930, and gone by 1940 (replaced by the Shell Gas Station in the Main/Humboldt photo on *page 66*.) This site, or close to it, had, in the 1830s, been the site of a toll gate, to help pay for the paving of Main Street.

View From the sidewalk in front of Dr. Hollway's office. George Zornick remembers Henry's Hamburgers, seen in the background in this 1977 shot. "It was a big deal when that opened (in 1967), especially within walking distance. For less than a dollar you could fill yourself up. It was kind of a destination for us, a full day for us. (Buffalo Bills player and Channel 2 Sportscaster) Ernie Warlick owned it, he was a big sports hero for us, and he'd work the counter every once in a while. We'd also take our spare change and hike over to the Central Park Plaza. They had all kinds of great '5 and dime' type stores there like Kresges, Murphys. We'd poke around in the stores all day, maybe grab something at the soda fountain, and that was a day for us." The Henry's Location is Tony's Ranch House today.

Through the 60s, 70s and 80s, the block of Main Street between Vernon Place and Orchard Place, near where Main Street and Fillmore Avenue meet, was a hot nightspot for the young set, and for jazz fans. Clubs and restaurants like The Casa Savoy, Dirty Dick's Bathhouse, and the original Tralfamadore Cafe were well-known places for music and partying.

In 1972, three North Buffalo brothers bought a vacant bar with a leaky roof on Main Street. It was the birth of a Parkside institution. The Stuffed Mushroom was born at the hands of Jim, Dennis, and Donald Alfieri at the corner of Main and Orchard Place, and remained for nearly three decades. They wanted to bring back the aura of the hot spot of the 40s and 50s at the same address, the "*Park Casino.*" The 1941 bar remained, and the brothers built out from around it. And they didn't stop at the walls of the Stuffed Mushroom.

The Alfieris were among the original organizers of the Main-Amherst Business Association, which is still active and partners with the

Like many memories, the Original Home of the Tralf is probably better in memory than it ever was in actual practice. Though hundreds of the world's finest jazz and off-beat music acts played the room, it was a cramped basement, accessible only by the steep staircase upon which workers are sitting during the club's last night. WEBR Jazz in the Nighttime Host Al Wallack, bottom center, broadcast live from the Tralf with great regularity.

Parkside Community Association as well as the Fillmore Leroy group, FLARE, and brother Jim was a director of the PCA. The Stuffed Mushroom closed in 1996.

For almost two centuries, Main Street-- and the goings-on on Main Street-- were inseparable from the goings-on in the Parkside neighborhood. As the 21st century enters its second decade, however, many who've lived in Parkside for a decade or more have never had reason to visit, walk on, or even drive through the portion of Main Street that has been the traditional backbone of the area. The slow, often painful changes that Main Street and the City of Buffalo experienced, and how the people of the Parkside area came to deal with them, are the integral part of the Parkside story that makes the community so unique among Buffalo neighborhoods.

Chapter 7: *The Decline and Rebirth of Parkside*

Main Street was the backbone of the Parkside neighborhood that was pretty well built out by about 1920; most structures built after then were built either on subdivided larger lots, or on lots where a previous structure was either burned or by some other means destroyed.

The 1920s were a wonderful time in the prosperous neighborhood.

Stately elm trees had started reaching maturity and formed a shady canopy over each of the streets of the neighborhood. A mix of horse-drawn trucks and motor vehicles carried men plying their wares from house to house. The glass bottles of the milkman clanked; groceries were left on porches; 25, 50, and 100 pound blocks of ice delivered in the summer; loads of coal dropped into basement chutes in the winter. Children looked forward to the more colorful bakery trucks, scissors grinders, and ragmen as they shouted and sang hoping the ladies of the houses might need their services.

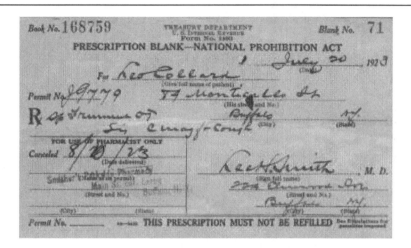

One noticeably absent diversion in Parkside, and the country, during the 1920's: The Neighborhood watering hole. Anyone desirous of legal booze had to belly up to the Pharmacy, like Smither's Parkside, with a script like this one from a doctor for 'Spiritus Fermentus.' Many Parkside homes saw wet bars, if not full blown speak easies, built in basements during this time.

These services were used and enjoyed with the sacrifices of war fresh in the minds of Americans. The Great War, as World War I was known until a greater war 30 years later, forced meatless Sundays, heatless Mondays, coaless Tuesdays, and wheatless dinners at Buffalo Hotels several times a week.

Late in the war, college students drafted into the Army were trained before shipping overseas right at their respective colleges. Canisius College holed up their recruits in special barracks put together at St Mary's School for the Deaf. Those student-soldiers drilled on the lawn right at Main and Jefferson Streets, on the lawn of the College's main building. The young men from Canisius were never needed overseas, and were all honorably discharged.

Student Army of Canisius College drill on the College Grounds, Main and Jefferson Streets. From the book Buffalo's Part in the World War

Falchaire, Noted French Ace, About to Land on Meadow at Delaware Park, 1918

But many did leave from Parkside for the fighting in Europe. A crowd of 50,000 jammed into the meadow at Delaware Park to bid farewell to 3,000 local soldiers on their way to battle with Germany's Kaiser. *The Buffalo Evening News* described the scene in June, 1917:

A full moon climbing through the heavy clouds gave the final touch of splendor to a setting which made the Meadow a fairyland. There was a touch of awed surprise in the attitude of the great crowd that filled the meadow to overflowing when the first note of music burst forth and song and light became one harmonious whole. Paths between the trees were transformed into lantern-lined vistas. The lanterns beckoned everywhere. They pointed the way for the throngs that flowed through every entrance toward the flowing center of the celebration.

The years that followed World War I, *The Roaring 20s,* were indeed a sort of golden time for Parkside even more than the rest of the nation; a prosperous decade that was to be followed by an especially rough decade and a half.

The Great Depression

The Parkside neighborhood of the 1920's was an upper middle class neighborhood; just the type of place that was hit hardest by the 1929 Wall Street Crash and the ensuing decade of economic depression. All over the country, the wealthier the individual, the harder they fell as depression struck. Jack and Wally Flett remembered the way the crippling economy changed their grocery business, which they ran on Russell Avenue, one door from the corner of Parkside Avenue, for over 50 years.

The best years of the business were the first years- *before the depression*- the Fletts remembered, when every home on Jewett Parkway had a chauffeur and a maid. The maid would call in an order, and the driver would come pick it up. That changed quickly, but the Fletts weren't complaining, knowing they were lucky to not lose everything. "We had a customer on Summit who was a millionaire one day, and a pauper the next. He had a huge account with the store, and though he was broke, he eventually paid every cent."

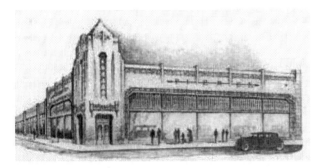

And it wasn't just the Fletts. The elegant, luxurious Pierce-Arrow Motor Company opened its brand new showroom at Main Street and Jewett Parkway just weeks before the market crashed in the fall of 1929. The company and the showroom languished for a few years, the economy had taken its toll, and by mid 30's, was selling Pontiacs and Cadillacs from the Art Deco automotive palace.

Just as Pierce-Arrow fell on hard times, so too, did many families of the Parkside neighborhood who drove those cars. At one time or another, Darwin D. Martin owned three Pierce-Arrows. By the time he died in 1935, he was comparatively

MAXSON
CADILLAC-PONTIAC
CORPORATION

penniless. Martin's son, Darwin R., had assumed control of the family's fortune, and heavily leveraged the fortune his father had created with a lifetime of hard work.

The younger Martin was described by a niece as "selfish," "a wheeler dealer," and "a hard drinking man." He was a real estate developer, who built the very stylish 800 West Ferry Street Apartment building (as of 2009, recently acquired by Canisius High School) and at one point ran the Stuyvesant Hotel on Elmwood Avenue. Within two years of the senior Darwin Martin's death, in 1937, the younger Martin had moved his mother into one of his apartment complexes, leaving the Frank Lloyd Wright "opus" at Jewett Parkway and Summit Avenue abandoned.

As the property fell into arrears on taxes through the '30s and '40s, the younger Martin made no effort to maintain the home; worse, he expedited the home's literal downfall. He removed all the doors and all of the lighting fixtures, as well as other original trappings and accessories from the home. These he installed in his other stylish properties like the Stuyvesant and 800 West Ferry. He also stripped the home of copper electrical wire and copper plumbing. Nine years after Mrs. Martin moved from the home, the City of Buffalo was the sole bidder at a foreclosure sale. The property was taken over for $76,468 in back taxes, and a $394.53 payment to Darwin R. Martin.

Parkside children of the late '30s, '40s, and early '50s remember the future landmark as a somewhat spooky and dangerous place to play hide and seek. Other kids took advantage of the smooth open floors to roller skate. The now-world-famous art glass windows and glass and tile fixtures were the stuff of target practice for stone throwing kids. The home remained neglected and vandalized until the mid-1950s.

The fate of the Darwin Martin house showed the extreme end of what happened to some of Parkside's homes during the period between World Wars. The lean times of the Depression, followed by the rationing and requisitioning of materials during the World War II years left many homes much worse for the wear. However, the ones who were in those homes- no matter how worn- knew they were the lucky ones. Parksiders of the Depression Era will remember smoke from hobo's winter fires wafting up over the bridges in the Park Gully.

Parkside Goes to War... Again.

"I can remember when, as we used to say, the *Japs* attacked Pearl Harbor. I was outside playing football," recalls Jack Anthony, who grew up Greenfield Avenue. "Bob Bickel, who lived at 121 Greenfield, came out and yelled, *'Hey, did you hear the Japs attacked Pearl Harbor?'* I was in sixth grade, and I said, *'What does that matter? You want to play football or don't you?'*"

The kids played football that day, but they, too, would contribute to the war effort. Jack Anthony, destined to become one of the founders of the Parkside Community Association, was a lad on Greenfield, and later on West Oakwood Place during the war years.

"We had a gang... We played at the Dewey Playground, and the Parkside Candy Shoppe. It was a real routine, the way real men went to a bar, we went to that candy shop. During the war, the government made us Junior Rangers," Anthony remembers. "We did tire drives and scrap drives, collecting metal scraps people left out, and newspapers. We filled up the back lot at School 54 with the stuff. The war was a part of our lives, part of my life."

An interesting time for children, but a trying time for adults. While the Depression years were hard for the Flett Brothers, the most difficult time for the brothers and their store came during World War II. "The government didn't think our store was an essential service, so we worked 'til 3 in the store, and then worked in a defense plant 'til midnight."

Mrs. Martha Lang, who lived in a flat on Crescent Avenue for over 50 years, remembered vividly both her own home and her mother's house just up the street on Humboldt Parkway in the 1940s. She shared some of her wartime memories of the neighborhood in a 1990 issue of the *Parkside News*.

During a particularly cold wartime winter, there were natural gas shortages, which sent Mrs. Lang to live at her mother's coal heated home for a week. Her apartment, however, had an electric range which forced her to shuttle back and forth to prepare and serve meals.

It was after all, wartime. Jack Anthony remembers, "We had an air raid drill here, and we stood out on the porch on Greenfield. I was really amazed at how dark it was, truly dark. No lights on anywhere. That's stayed with me. And I took a walk once with my father to School 64 on Amherst St, because he had to register for the draft. He was 42 years old."

Anthony remembers Saturday afternoons at the Central Park show, where Main Street and Fillmore Avenue meet. "I was just a kid, but I sure knew I hated *Japs*. We'd watch the newsreels, and the American Soldier would stand at the edge of a cave with a flame thrower, and with a *woosh* we'd cheer in the movie house, *Get those bastards!* and then we'd go wild cheering when Japs'd run out on fire. I had a job done on me in terms of propaganda, but I never knew it."

While those newsreels showed the war being fought in exotic locations, little did young Jack Anthony (or anyone else, at that time) know that groundbreaking, top secret Government work was being done right in Parkside, right in the old Ford Plant.

America's First Jet Plane: Parkside Built.

With the war at full tilt, and America on the brink of entering on the side of the Allies, Larry Bell had fallen asleep listening to an Indians night game on the radio. He was awakened by his wife with a phone call from Washington. The Pentagon was on the line, and Larry and his top engineer would be on a train to the nation's capital by midnight.

On September 5, 1941, Bell Aircraft entered into a top secret agreement to begin producing the first American versions of the world's first jet aircraft. Up until this point, no American plane -ever- had flown without the whir of a propeller. Bell would produce the planes; GE, the engines. With no one sure what the Japanese and Germans were up to, speed was a priority. By the end of the month, a $1.6 million contract was signed to build three of the as-yet-designed jet planes.

The design work on three different aircraft began on the train trip back to Buffalo, and by the next morning, the site for the design and manufacture of the aircraft was decided. The Ford Motor factory, on Main Street in Buffalo, had been mothballed when the company's manufacturing operations moved to Woodlawn ten years earlier. The last remaining vestige of Ford at the building, a Ford Dealer and Sales Agency on the ground floor, was moved out overnight.

Now the TriMain building, the hulking red brick structure undertook a quick makeover to make in an appropriate home for one of the war efforts' most secretive projects up until that point. The windows were welded shut; a special pass was needed to get past the sentry which guarded the location twenty-four hours a day. The security was on-par with that surrounding the Manhattan Project, and it was all in Parkside.

As the FBI began screening production workers for the top secret job, "Drinkers, bar-room talkers, and womanizers were ruled out as risks." The ground floor was made into a machine shop, assembly on the second floor. Some components that had to be made at other Bell plants were given false names; an exhaust pipe might be labeled a heater duct.

The work force at Main Street and Rodney Avenue were mostly selected as the best of Bell's other factories. Donald Norton wrote of it *Larry: A Biography of Lawrence D. Bell*:

> (P)eople began to disappear at the Elmwood and Wheatfield plants. A lathe operator or draftsman would come to work in the morning and find that the man next to him suddenly had been replaced by somebody new.
>
> "Hey!" one machine operator exclaimed. "What happened to Harry?"
>
> "I got told this morning to come over here," was the reply. "Who's Harry?"
>
> Men excused themselves from car pools with a standard reply that sounded almost too casual. "Just assigned to a temporary job. No Sweat. Be back in the pool in a couple of months." One car pool group went to plant security with the suspicion that a recent dropout may have fled with secret papers.
>
> Employees engaged on the XP-59A project could not tell their families what they were working on or where they were working. If a family emergency arose, the spouse would call an unlisted number. The operator at the Main Street facility would take the information, send it by guard to the employee, and then the employee placed a separate call home.

Work began on the "XP-59A" in early 1942. It was so designated to give the impression that this new venture was simply an improvement of the XP-59 propeller craft. On August 4, 1942, the first engine arrived at the plant via the beltline railway. Security was ratcheted tighter. On September 10, workers began removing bricks from the wall of the building, facing the rail lines, so that crates containing the aircraft's fuselage and wings could be lowered onto railcars bound for testing grounds in California's Mojave Desert. America's first jet was successfully flown September 30, 1942. It had been about a year since the phone call during the baseball game.

In March 1943, a second, improved XP-59A was shipped from Buffalo for testing, this one wrapped in canvas, with a mock propeller attached to the front of the craft to disguise the generally unthinkable jet propulsion ability of the craft.

Eventually, 50 P-59 aircraft were built for use by the Army and Navy. They weren't used in combat, but mostly for testing and training. It was written in the Government's summary of the program in June, 1945, that, "Even though a combat airplane did not result... the development was very worthwhile, since it proved the principle of jet propulsion for aircraft was sound and practical." The work in Buffalo provided the ground work for the US's venture into the jet age.

Planes were moved about with artificial propellers attached, to disavow any thought that the plane was powered by jet propulsion.

As quickly as Bell swept into the old Ford Plant, the aerospace giant left when it no longer needed the extra space. But, in May 1942, the Navy enjoyed the fruits of Parkside's wartime labor as the Hercules Motor Corporation began building diesel engines at the plant, and did so through the end of the war. After the war, The Trico Products Company manufactured windshield wiper components at the building for the next 3 ½ decades.

A (Vice) Presidential Visit

As the war continued to churn, Harry Truman's last public appearance before becoming President upon the death of Franklin D. Roosevelt came in Parkside, specifically, at the Episcopal Church of the Good Shepherd. Truman worshipped there April 8, 1945.

According to "Forth," the Diocesan news magazine, and as chronicled in *A Century in The Fold: A History of The Church of the Good Shepherd*, The Vice President was in Buffalo to make a speech at a Democratic

Dinner at the Hotel Statler on April 7. Truman's friend, tour guide, Buffalo Democrat, and Good Shepherd Warden Charles Diebold, Jr, surprised the congregation by bringing the Vice President for services.

After introducing Truman to children at the Sunday school, Diebold asked him to autograph a copy of the church bulletin. But the always wry Vice President responded with, "I usually do the autographing, but this time I want you to do it; and I'm going to present this autographed bulletin to Mrs. Truman to show her that I attended church today." Four days later, he was President of the United States. A month later, the war in Europe ended. 4 months later, the war in the Pacific ended when President Truman decided to use atomic weapons against Japan.

Which brings us back to Jack Anthony-- he remembers the end of the war as well as the beginning of it. Four long years after it started, he wasn't busy playing football when he heard the war ended. "In 1945, when it ended, I walked all the way downtown from here. For the celebration, I guess, I don't know. I didn't kiss any nurses or drink any beer; I just walked downtown to see it."

The war years were difficult in Parkside, as they were all over the nation. According to the 1947 accounting of Buffalo's 1,835 war dead in the *Buffalo Evening News Almanac,* no less than 22 *mostly young* men who listed a Parkside home address died overseas. On the home front, it was during World War II that many large single family homes were sub-divided into apartments to meet the growing demand for housing for war-effort factory workers. The Federal Government declared Buffalo a "Labor Shortage Area" in 1942. But once the war ended, production fell quickly.

Adults were left without jobs, and children were left without the organized activities of the war. In his book *Coming of Age in Buffalo: Youth and Authority in the Postwar Era*, William Graebner talks about the growing problem of juvenile delinquency in the early 1950s:

> *In the fall of 1953, Buffalo Police and magistrates began to enforce a city ordinance against "corner lounging," a relatively innocuous if irritating activity believed to have some relationship to more advanced forms of delinquent behavior. Police made arrests at Cazenovia and Seneca, French and Fillmore, Broadway and Madison, Louisiana and South Park, and the 2600 block of Main Street. (That's in the vicinity of Main and Fillmore on the east; between Orchard and Amherst on the west side of Main.)*

Graebner quotes the Babcock Precinct Captain McNamara as saying, "Bring these adolescent apes into the station and don't treat them gently. These punks have more respect for a cop's night stick than for the entire Code of Criminal Procedure." He also writes that the church began playing an increasing role in the social needs of postwar youth, sponsoring parish dances and, later sock hops.

> *In North Buffalo, the Friday-night parish dances rotating among St. Margaret's Holy Spirit, St Vincent's, (and St. Mark's) were the most important social events of the weekend, and not just for Catholics. "Back in those days, " recalls one resident, the CYO (Catholic Youth Organization) was the big thing."*

As you've already read, the *powers that be* also made sure that the younger set had to snap to strict guidelines. School 54, the public elementary school on Main Street across from Leroy Avenue, started its day with a prayer in the 1950s, but also found it a necessity to ban "slacks for girls, and dungarees for all pupils." And while corporal punishment was still meted out with some regularity, some thought children were "getting away easy" without long-time principal Clara Swartz roaming the halls with her rubber hose, for use on errant students.

What the newly christened "teenagers" were doing didn't matter to some anyway. By the early 1950s, many men who'd fought in Europe and the Pacific had already graduated from college and other training paid for by the GI Bill. Those better educated men wanted something better than the tired city in which they were raised. The depopulation of the city for the suburbs was underway, and city leaders were literally making it easier to leave-- via ribbons of asphalt highway.

"Urban Renewal"

After the war, people wanted to leave the worn city behind, in favor of bright, clean, shiny new suburbs. And what better way to get people to the suburbs than 4 and 6 lane divided highways.

The original thought was enthusiastic, but, as later admitted, misguided. Planners said when the population along the Niagara Frontier reaches 1.5 million, 2 million, 3 million... People spread all over Western New York will want to get Downtown quickly for the best entertainment, for the glitziest shopping, for the finest restaurants, and, of course, to work. "Suburban traffic," it was written in the 1946 report *The New York State*

Thruway and Arterial Routes in the Buffalo Urban Area, "must be given high consideration in the logical treatment of any conditions in the city."

There was very little resistance to this idea to prepare Buffalo for the bold new future. The Parkside neighborhood was at the center of the plan that would turn Buffalo into the *20 minute city* it continues to be.

There was a much different aesthetic in the days before six lanes of highway made an abrupt incision in the landscape. Parkside's southerly border was and is Humboldt Parkway, but the pre-1960 Humboldt Parkway was a far cry from what it is today. *(see photo below)*

The street was designed by Olmsted to connect *The Park* (Delaware Park) to *the Parade* (later Humboldt Park, now Martin Luther King Park) in such a way that one could travel from one to the other without feeling like they left a park at all. Once, eight rows of stately trees stood on the 200-foot wide median between the two sides of the divided parkway.

At Delaware Park, Humboldt Parkway ended at Agassiz Circle, with the grand entrance to Park. The Parkway continued with the gracefully curved, two-lane Scajaquada Parkway. Young people would often pull off the road to "park" under the statue of David, or toboggan in the winter.

Mrs. Martha Lang, who lived on Crescent Avenue for over 50 years, remembered vividly her mother's home on Humboldt Parkway in the 1940s. Speaking with the Parkside News in 1990, she called Humboldt's tree-shaded median "a place for lovers to stroll, kids to play, to sit on your front porch and watch the passing scene." She lamented its loss, and said the whole character of the area changed when the Scajaquada Expressway took its place.

In 1953, with the north/south 190 already in place, planners released plans for a series of 5 east/west highways to bisect the city and increase the ability for traffic to move in and out of downtown, with no waiting in heavy city traffic.

One of the proposals seemed like a fait accompli. Unlike the others, which cut through neighborhoods, this cut through land described by planners as "vacant." Four years later, in 1957, that "vacant" land that was the middle of Delaware Park became home to a high speed thoroughfare. The Scajaquada Creek Expressway opened as a widened, jersey-barriered and guard-railed 50 mile-an-hour version of the sleepy, winding 15 mile-an-hour path that once stood in the same place.

Creating the Elmwood/198 offramp, 1958

To meet up with the planned Kensington Expressway, The Scajaquada Expressway was extended past the footprint of the old Scajaquada Parkway, right through the beginning of Humboldt Parkway to about Delevan Avenue. Humboldt Parkway was at grade level with Main Street. The blasting that took place to sink the roadway to 20 feet below grade, and expose the walls of Onondaga limestone, rattled picture frames off of walls throughout the neighborhood, just as the blasting out of the Beltline did 50 years before, and blasting out of the *MetroRail* would 30 years later.

As the Kensington and Scajaquada Expressways were built, Agassiz Circle, once the stately, grand entrance to Delaware Park, all but disappeared. No longer a parkway divided by grass and trees, Humboldt Parkway became two parallel one way streets separated by six lanes of blown out-sunken in asphalted expressway. The city encroachment that Olmsted designed Parkside to eliminate was here.

But believe or not, it really could have been worse. In his 1983 book *High Hopes*, Mark Goldman outlines a 1958 proposal for another expressway, thankfully never built, called the *Delaware Park Shortway*. It would have "taken a large chunk of Delaware Park meadow and built there yet another divided highway, across the park and parallel to the Scajaquada."

Traffic didn't move for days on Rte 198 in late January/early February 1977, as Parkside and the Buffalo area dealt with the deadly Blizzard of '77.

Aside from the new Scajaquada Expressway going through the middle of it, The Delaware Park Meadow went through some other changes as well. The golf course was laid out around the turn of the century, and fully constructed in 1930. The Park Superintendent's house, "The Farmstead," built in 1875, was torn down in 1950 to make way for the current Zoo parking lot. And the stone garden-- a quarried-out area behind the Parkside Lodge at Florence, filled with plants and flowers-- was filled in to make way for a par 3 golf hole after a child was found dead in the pond at the bottom of the pit.

But it wasn't just politicians and city planners who changed the Parkside landscape in the 1950s and 60s. Mother Nature, too, landed a body blow to the trees of the neighborhood, when Dutch Elm disease struck.

Over 10,000 trees died of Dutch Elm disease in the City of Buffalo, many hundreds in Parkside. Up until the early 1960s, every street in the neighborhood was covered with a canopy of elm branches. By the mid 1960s, it became clear that the battle to save the trees was a losing one.

In the earliest days of the Parkside Community Association, one of its major concerns was the dying trees. The first item in the April, 1966 newsletter for the group dealt with the trees, and seemed to be grasping at straws.

> *SAVE YOUR ELMS -- It is evident that we are losing the fight against Dutch Elm disease. The chemical Bidrin which offered hope a year ago has not proved itself and is now not being used.*

> *The only safe and effective treatment is the special DDT spray which must be used before the leaves unfold in the spring. Davey Tree Experts and United Tree Surgeons are among the firms under "Tree Service" in the yellow pages which are known to offer this service. Spraying equipment, however, is limited and there are not many days left which are clear and calm enough to apply the spray.*

> <u>NOW</u> *is the time to order this service if you want to SAVE YOUR ELMS.*

Jewett Pkwy in the 1930s, when its elm trees were at their peak, before dying of Dutch elm disease in the 60s.

But not even the later-to-be-found carcinogenic DDT was enough to stop the spread of the disease. It was well into the '80s and '90s before a concerted city-initiated effort would begin to replace the hundreds of trees that had fallen to the blight, and changed the character of the neighborhood forever.

Social Upheaval

Despite the fact that suburban flight had begun, most who grew up in Parkside in the 50s and 60s describe it as a *Leave It to Beaver,* idyllic place to live and grow up. "We left our doors unlocked. Break-ins were unheard of. It seemed every other house had kids our age. There were always pickup games in the street...Football, baseball... and even though we used a tennis ball we still broke a few windows. It wouldn't be unusual to get 20 boys together to play football or tag in someone's backyard."

But each of those 20 boys was white. The streets of Parkside were populated almost entirely, with only rare exception, by whites. "It's not like there were fights in the streets, but when black kids rode their bikes through the neighborhood it was noticed. It was still a pretty lily white neighborhood."

Most kids knew that it wasn't smart to travel outside of your own neighborhood by yourself at that time. Long glares from the kids of the strange neighborhood you were visiting was likely the best treatment you could expect. But in Parkside, it was painfully obvious that if you were black and passing through, you didn't belong.

As a man who later fought vigorously to bring the races together in Parkside and in Buffalo as a whole, Jack Anthony graphically remembers the somewhat unusual sight of black children as he grew up in Parkside in the 1940s. "Sometimes we'd see black kids in the park, on their 'nigger bikes.' That's what we called them. Some of the black kids had these bikes with a couple of horns, a couple of headlights, all jazzed up. We never thought white kids would do that. And we hated those kids, and we hated those bikes."

Racial differences and problems weren't the only under bubbling current. Ethnic and religious bigotry was also more widely socially acceptable. Anthony recalls his high school experience, just north of the Parkside neighborhood.

When I was a freshman at Bennett (early 1950s), we had race riots. It was Jewish kids and non-Jewish kids... There were no blacks there then, so it was, as we used to say then, white kids being up Jewish kids, and vice versa. Isn't that sick? One of the ministers from Central (Presbyterian Church at Main and Jewett), a rabbi, and a priest all came to an assembly talking to us all about being better citizens. I can remember a bunch of friends leaving a "Hi-Y" High School YMCA meeting and head up to Hertel to find a bunch of "kikes" to beat up. That was the mentality. But by the end of my four years at Bennett, relations between the Jewish kids and non-Jewish kids had greatly improved. One of my best friends, a Jewish kid, got beaten up pretty badly. I often wondered whether it was my other friend and his crew who may have done it.

But by the early 1960's, the situation was changing. "Urban Renewal" projects, like the building of the Kensington Expressway, were destroying the neighborhoods inhabited by middle-class upwardly mobile black families. Displaced, many were attempting to make Parkside, and other predominately white middle class neighborhoods, their home.

Some unscrupulous businessman played on the fears of whites that their neighborhood was "going black." The result in many Buffalo neighborhoods, including Parkside, was red-lining and blockbusting.

Redlining is an effort on the part of people in the banking and insurance industries to increase the price of, or deny services based on geographic location. *Blockbusting* was a scheme involving real estate agents putting families under pressure to sell their homes "before the neighborhood goes bad." Both were an effort to destroy neighborhoods by buying cheap, selling high, and playing on the fears of people living in a changing city and changing society while reaping profits.

In 1963, four black families lived in Parkside. At least one real estate agent began calling their neighbors, speaking vaguely of perspective buyers, and the fact that they should sell while they can. Panic reigned, and several people, affiliated with a neighboring church, pooled resources to buy a house from underneath a black family looking to move into the area.

In May 1963, a community meeting was held at St. Mark Church to discuss all manner of topics affecting the neighborhood. After a long discussion of a proposed North Buffalo Ice Rink, lifelong Parkside resident Jack Anthony asked the group's thoughts on black families moving into the area. Discussion was immediately cut off, and the topic deemed "too controversial."

Flabbergasted, Anthony and Richard Griffin organized a community meeting to discuss race in Parkside. At the time, the neighborhood was very diverse in almost every way: A mix of all ages, religions, educational backgrounds, and economic conditions. Anthony and Griffin agreed that while it hadn't yet, racial diversity should also come to Parkside in a way that it didn't around the rest of the city. The Parkside Community Association (PCA) was formed, and on July 1, 1963, an 8 page outline of what the group stood for was distributed around the neighborhood. An excerpt from that original PCA Newsletter follows:

> *We feel there is a real need for this to maintain and improve our wonderful area.... (At our first meeting), a very frank and fruitful discussion occurred. It was agreed that no useful purpose would be served by an extended argument over the integration of this particular part of the city. Integration present and future is a fact. Four Negro families presently own or occupy homes. More persons of a minority race will no doubt purchase homes in the near future. This is their right as it should be any person's right to reside where he chooses. No one is opposed to anyone residing in our community because of his race or religion.*

> *What the group wants for this neighborhood is to make it the best possible place to live -- to raise our families, to obtain an education, to grow intellectually, spiritually, and physically. We want good neighbors regardless of color. We want all to stay and continue to live where we live. We want to attract persons of all ages, religions, races, education, economic abilities, etc to move our fine community. We want to preserve the area's residential character. We are proud of our public and parochial schools and of our well kept houses, trees, lawns, shrubs, and yards. We like to live in the City of Buffalo among its fine families and with the urban conveniences we enjoy. We think that no area offers as much housing for a reasonable price as the property which we are fortunate to own. We desire not only to preserve these values but to improve our particular community so that it is a model of responsible urban life.*

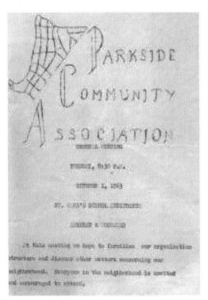

While interested in more than just open housing, the PCA had to move quickly to counter-act the unscrupulous real estate agents and others looking to profit from the fears of others. Scare tactics were used to try to get people to sell, rumors of neighbors selling their homes spread had spread like wildfire. The PCA stepped up to stop the illegal division of single family homes into multiple units, which helped stem sales. They also drummed out real estate agents and others using unethical practices for their

An early PCA meeting announcement flyer, 1963

own gain at the cost of the neighborhood.

The likable and outgoing personalities of Griffin and Anthony helped them bring neighbors aboard and their activity in St. Mark and Central Presbyterian churches respectively helped bring those institutions and the clergy at those two institutions, in line with the process.

Jack Anthony has, over the years, related this story with the original language in tact to underline the types of people he would come against. The Reverend James Carroll listened to one angry congregant at Central Presbyterian. "The first time a nigger comes into this church and sits down next to me, I'm leaving." Rev. Carroll was quick to reply, very calmly, "Let me shake your hand now then, because I'm not coming out of the pulpit to say goodbye to you when that happens."

It was under conditions such as these that the Mesiahs were among those first four black families to own a home in Parkside. Frank Mesiah, later to become an original PCA Board Member, and President of the Buffalo Chapter of the NAACP, was interviewed by Ruth Lampe for an article that appeared in the September 1988 issue of *The Parkside News*.

In 1961...(The Mesiahs) forced to leave their Humboldt-Delevan home because of the construction of the Kensington Expressway.... When Frank told a real estate agent in a telephone conversation that he was a policeman and teacher, he immediately assumed he was white and made an appointment to show him homes in North Buffalo. But when he appeared at the office, the agent went into a panic and, after much double talk, he ended up never showing Frank any homes. Finally, a black realtor helped them find a new home on Crescent Avenue...

He recalls experiencing some hostility from some residents and tells of a few parents who wouldn't let the Mesiah daughters play at their houses. But he also remembers that those people's children would sneak down to play at the Mesiah's. He can also laugh now, remembering people offering him shoveling jobs while he was shoveling snow outside of his new home, or people asking is wife, "Is the lady of the house in?", when she answered the door.

Frank also admits he felt somewhat suspicious when "all of the sudden this neighborhood organization comes up to 'preserve the neighborhood'." But after meeting with Dick Griffin and Jack Anthony, he was convinced of their sincerity and developed confidence in them. He came to understand they were reacting to talk that predominantly black areas didn't get proper garbage pick-up, different things were allowed to happen to the houses, and absentee landlords increased. "PCA wanted to be sure that things like that didn't happen here."

Mesiah himself would spearhead efforts to eradicate blockbusting from the neighborhood. The November, 1967 Parkside Newsletter read, "Mr. Mesiah reported on a contact with Genesee Realty Co. with respect to a certain notice sent. The representative of the Genesee Realty said that they would desist from sending these in our community. The 1965 PCA Report to members included this piece of information:

Real Estate: Three of the officers of the Association recently met with a real estate agent whose company was alleged to have called two residents of a street in our area where a house has been purchased by a Negro. The agent was most cooperative in questioning his staff, and although he was convinced that no salesman in his office made the calls, he assured us that none will ever be made from his office under such conditions. If any resident is ever contacted by a real estate salesman who urges sale because of non-white neighbors, get the agent's name and address. Contact Jack Anthony or Dick Griffin with this information so that appropriate legal action may be initiated by the Association against such a salesman, in this way we will continue to let it be known that our area is not available for block busting.

But of course, not everyone felt this way. One resident remembers, "Parkside was a white neighborhood, and there were plenty of people who wanted to keep it that way. While it may have not been a plank in the PCA, one of the reasons for the growth of the group was the hope that it would help keep Parkside white. Now that may have been a misunderstanding, but that's how many people thought."

"It was a common thing to hear in the neighborhood; when someone was selling, 'You're selling to the whites, right?' and when white people moved in, 'Glad you moved in.' It wasn't screaming racism, but it was understood that we should want to keep the area white. Right in the front of many people's minds is what happened in the Central Park Plaza area (just across Main Street.) It was once a nice, working class neighborhood, then, seemingly over night, 'it went, you know...'"

But, all and all, an even-handed approach made Parkside a continued desirable area for people of all races; not an accomplishment that most city neighborhoods could boast of, even as time wore on. Many leaders of the WNY African-American community, either by deed or office, have made Parkside home over the ensuing years. Frank Mesiah and his family have lived on Crescent since 1961. Longtime Deputy Speaker of the New York State Assembly Arthur O. Eve, Jr. raised his 5 children on Jewett Parkway.

Two trailblazers in the world of athletics have also called Parkside home. Willie Evans, the UB Football star halfback, who was denied the right to play in the 1958 Tangerine Bowl because of his race, lived in Parkside for over 30 years. Jim Thorpe, the first black man to ever lead a PGA Major when he took the lead of the 1981 US Open, lived on Parkside Avenue for most of the 1980s, and could often be seen hitting golf balls in Delaware Park.

School Integration: Parkside School #54

It was the desire and goal of many in the neighborhood that families

 with the means to buy a home in Parkside, regardless of their race, should be allowed to live freely and be a welcome part of the community. But home life was only one part of the clash between the races in Buffalo in the 1960s and 70s.

"White flight" was caused in many areas of the city when the racial balance at public schools in the neighborhood changed in a matter of a year or two. Once again, this situation presented itself in Parkside at School 54, which has stood on Main Street since 1895.

Just as the Parkside Community Association fought blockbusting, it also worked to make schools racially balanced. When the association was formed, 2 of its original 5 goals dealt directly with maintaining and building upon the success of the school. 54 was already enjoying a rebirth of sorts. As the PCA was founded in 1963, plans were already in the works for a new school to be built. A PCA newsletter from January, 1964, includes a building update, and an update on the group's early lobbying efforts.

> *Demolition work has been completed at the new site of School 54... The Board of Education (has abandoned) the voluntary student transfer plan because it was not in the best interests of maintaining racial balance at the school.*

The new (current) school would open in 1965, built on the property that was once Hagner's Dairy. The former building stood to the left of the current one; the site where School 54 stood from 1895-1964 now serves as the school's parking lot.

In 1958, Matthew Duggan became principal at School 54, still housed in the old building. Mr. Duggan's leadership through some rough times, and the strong participation of parents and the community, helped keep School 54 a "*showcase school*" while many of the city's other schools deteriorated through the 1960s and beyond.

But making sure that new building remained one of the city's finest schools was no small task. Many Parksiders, both parents, and PCA members, lobbied City Hall and Albany to gain better funding for the school, and to help maintain racial balance at the school.

A 1962 survey of Buffalo schools by the NAACP sets the scene. 17 Buffalo Public schools are listed as "Negro schools," with at least 60% of its pupils black. 14 of those 17 had at least 90% black students. There were 47 "White schools," with 19 having 100% white enrollment, and 28 more having 95%-99% white pupils.

Only 16 schools were listed as "integrated," and 11 of those schools had an African-American enrollment of less than 20%. Parkside's School 54 was one of only 5 schools in the city where blacks and whites approached even numbers. In 1958, 11% of students were black. 39% of students were black in 1960. By 1964, the number had grown to 54%.

A racially diverse 1961 School 54 class photo.

This came about through a number of different factors. The school was a part of an early desegregation trial, where parents in one east side neighborhood were given the option of having their children bussed to the more academically solid School 54, rather than walking to their own neighborhood elementary school. Many parents chose this option, and the number of African-American children attending school in Parkside grew.

In a vacuum, the experiment might have been a success. But just as some families succumbed to the blockbusting attempts by scrupulous real estate salesmen, some saw the increased black enrollment at 54 as a threat to their children's education and placed their kids in the neighborhood Catholic parochial school at St. Mark's at Woodward and Amherst. In 1953, there were 40 1st graders at St Mark's. A decade later, in 1964, the number had more than doubled to 88.

There was hope, however, in the construction of the new school. The dilapidated, outdated classic 1890s school house had been a worn-out collection of hodge-podge additions and classrooms literally created from closets for years. The bright new plant promised a pleasant atmosphere for learning, and plus a wonderful school yard and playground.

In May, 1965, letter to parents of school aged kids; the Parkside Community Association outlined the hope for a new school with a sense of hope and optimism. Schools Committee Chairman Saul Touster wrote, "It is our expectation... That there will be a migration of students from... St. Marks into School 54, especially in the lower grades."

The tone was decidedly different in a letter Touster wrote to State Education Commissioner James Allen from the Community Association a month earlier:

> (T)his school, instead of being considered a positively integrated school, must now be considered a school whose racial <u>imbalance</u> threatens to make it a de facto segregated school. The inclusion of an optional area for the school's district has had the effect of concentrating upon School 54 the pressure for integrated education for the negro community. It is in no one's interest that a school be pressured until it "topples over." If balance cannot be maintained here at a school where community reception of integration has been so positive and community interest continues to be so willing, then the larger problems will become hopeless of solution.

While there were parallels to be drawn between housing integration in the Parkside Neighborhood, and the school integration in School 54, there were, however, some key differences as well.

Michael Riester, who'd grow up to be a historian, social worker, and President of the Parkside Community Association, was in the mid 1960s, a kid on West Oakwood Place and a pupil at School 54. "It was a neighborhood school. The majority of the kids were from the neighborhood, from both sides of Main Street, and both white and black."

But when Riester was in 5th grade, in 1966, things changed. There was a fire at School 17, on Delevan Avenue near Main Street. 130 mostly poor, and all black students were "temporarily transferred" to 54. The addition of these children pushed the ratio of black students to almost 80%, a statistic that the PCA knew only added fuel to the fire that blockbusters were trying to create.

"It seemingly happened overnight," Riester recalls."(School 54) went from a neighborhood school, to a school that integrated kids from very different economic situations and cultural situations. You had poor black kids coming from the Fruit Belt, coming to 54 with kids from the neighborhood who were privileged. It was violent, a very difficult time. The tension in the school and in the classroom was racially charged. These kids were very angry. Now, I understand why they were angry; why they were frustrated. I'm not sure I did then."

It was in this atmosphere that some long established Parkside families moved to the suburbs, and many who didn't move, considered options other than Buffalo Public Schools for the education of their children. Among that second group: The Riesters.

"There was a boy who was a few years ahead of me, who lived on Crescent, who was stabbed at the corner of West Oakwood and Main, so badly he was hospitalized. My mother seriously thought about pulling me out and putting me in a parochial school. I remember her saying we could get you into St Joes or Holy Spirit. But I wound up staying at 54 until 7th grade."

"It was a foreign environment for me, certainly, and for many kids who lived in the neighborhood. It increased our fear of the unknown; the violence that we experienced, that I experienced, did not help me understand what the black experience was, and it was very frightening."

A Young Mike Riester, on the steps of his family's West Oakwood Place home, late 1950s.

Looking back, Riester knows. "These kids had nothing, and they were being thrown in with these wealthy white kids, who didn't know what it was like to show up at school hungry. The teachers must have understood, but were overwhelmed.

"When school was let out you would have fights. It was primarily, from what I remember, was black against white. I was beat up at least twice. What was ironic, it happened two blocks away from my home. I lived two blocks from school and couldn't make it home some days. It increased the fear of Main Street.

"It was a strange time. For the hour after school let out, you knew you were going to get beaten up if you didn't run home. But then, within two hours, your neighborhood returned. I don't even know if our parents really realized the extent of what was going on in school and right afterwards.

"I don't think anyone would challenge the statement that integration at School 54 wasn't a well thought-out process for any of the kids, for white kids and black kids."

One of the early concrete victories of the Association came after years of work by folks like PCA Board members Saul Touster, Richard

Griffin, Jim Barry, and Jack Anthony. In 1967, the State Education department awarded a $100,000 grant for 54 to develop a "superior program at the school to encourage families not to move out of the district." Those funds were used to cut class size, hire additional staff, provide enrichment and remediation programs, and pay for a preschool program for 4 year olds.

These programs were enough to make many Parkside families consider School 54 for their children. After a decade-high of 85 kindergarteners at St Mark's School in 1965, only 65 kindergarteners signed up for the 1968-69 school year.

But with the late 1960s questions of race and integration were no longer just the fodder of letters and public meetings. The frustrations of the African-American community were boiling over onto the streets, shocking and worrying some of the most ardent supporters of racial harmony and equality in Parkside.

Again, Mike Riester shares his memories. "I can remember sitting with other neighbors on my porch listening to gunfire, because the (infamous June/July, 1967) riots had come up as far as Jefferson and Delevan, only a few blocks to the south and east. Across from the Health Sciences Building at Canisius, there was a gun store, and the rioters had taken over the gun store. I can remember hearing the shotguns. The blasts. That was really frightening.

"My grandmother was at Sisters Hospital during the time. My father walked up to the hospital to visit her (from our home on West Oakwood Place near Crescent Avenue), and I can remember my mother being worried that he'd be attacked. That's the fear. That's how charged those times were.

"When Martin Luther King was assassinated (in 1968), we were let out of school early because they feared violence. I remember being told, 'Run home. Now Michael, run home.' That's the environment we were in."

The world was changing, too. Riester recalls that Main Street was becoming a place you didn't want to go, and it was also about the time a child was abducted from his Jewett Parkway yard, and later found dead in Delaware Park. "I can remember my parents telling me, 'You're not to go to the park anymore.' We couldn't go to the park unless we were in a large group. We couldn't go to the zoo anymore, even though it was free. It was the overall loss of innocence. It was like Camelot came crashing down. And it was happening all over the country, and it hit Parkside, too.

"That's not to say we weren't kids. We played outside all day and all night, until the street lights came on. But we were instilled with a little fear of some things. But it was a very normal childhood. There *were* black kids, and Asian kids, and white kids, but we all were neighborhood kids, and that was the important thing.

"All things told, I think Parkside handled integration very well. I remember when the first black family moved on my street, West Oakwood. Dr. Champion and his family. I became friends with the kids right off the bat. We obviously knew there was a difference in the color of our skin, but there I was in their home as often as they played on my porch. I don't remember any racial thoughts among us kids; I'm sure we worked it out in our own children's way. I remember adults saying things, but because integration was a gradual process in Parkside, it was easier. Many of the families who moved to Parkside in the 60s, both black and white, are still here."

"What was key was many of the families who moved into Parkside, the black families, were really no different from the white families socially and economically, culturally. I never remember any fights or violence happening in the neighborhood. It happened at school, but not in the neighborhood."

In 1976, Federal Judge John T. Curtin accused city leaders of "creating, maintaining, permitting, condoning, and perpetuating racially segregated schools in the City of Buffalo," and therefore ordered desegregation. School 54 was, as far as federal guidelines were concerned at this point, a segregated school with nearly 70% black enrollment.

A headline in the *Buffalo Evening News* at the time said *Struggle for Stability At School 54 Watched As a Cameo of Hope.* Many Parkside residents, lead by PTA (and later PCA) President Ruth Lampe, fought vehemently to keep the school integrated. Ruth and her husband David sent their two boys to the school. Lampe spent many hours fighting rumors and misconceptions about 54 and Buffalo Public Schools in general. Many of her Parkside neighbors recall Lampe's "won't take no for an answer" tactics in insuring that they send their children to the neighborhood public school, and not one of the area parochial schools.

Meetings and open discussions on the issues facing 54 were lead by Board of Education Member Florence Baugh, Delaware Common Councilman Harlan Swift, and the co-Chairmen of the Citizens' Council on Human Relations, Frank Mesiah and Norman Goldfarb. Mirroring the strong

PTA of the 1920s, a similar group in the 70s and 80s pushed forward an agenda that helped keep School 54 at the top of the class. Parkside residents Shirley Blickensderfer, Elva Radice, Marquerita Bell, Eileen Wagner, Chet Brodnicki, Jo Faber, Nancy Keech, Pat Schuder, Lori Lynch and numerous others were among those making sure the school received the parental, financial, political support it needed.

The story of School 54 could have easily been different without the legion of people interested in a strong school, and the strong in-school leadership of Principal Matthew Duggan and Sal Criscione (and their reciprocating concern for the neighborhood of which the school was a part). It is the school, in so many ways, that helped keep Parkside from slipping into the problems facing so man other fine city neighborhoods.

In 1980, School 54 became an Early Childhood Learning Center Magnet School, teaching grades Pre-K through 2. The school currently bears the name "Dr. George E. Blackman School of Excellence Early Childhood Center #54," named in honor of the one-time Buffalo School Board President who spoke up fiercely for the type of teaching done at the school, whose current mission statement reads:

> To create a school environment in which all children can learn. Our mission is to deliver instruction which is developmental, challenging, and success oriented.

As of 2009, the school is slated for massive renovation in Phase 4 of the Buffalo Schools on-going $1 billion reconstruction project.

Ideological Shift

Parkside's longstanding reputation as a politically conservative area predated the carving out of the neighborhood by Frederick Law Olmsted. The Granger Family, the first long-term white settlers in the area, was originally sent here with political patronage jobs from Thomas Jefferson. The Granger family's stone mansion on property that it now a part of Forest Lawn Cemetery was long known as the site of dozens of Republican fundraisers from the time of Lincoln up to the 1930s. Elam Jewett was a close friend of the Buffalo's Whig President Millard Fillmore. Before moving to what is now the corner of Jewett Parkway and Main Street, Jewett was the publisher of the very conservative and staid *Commercial Advertiser*, Buffalo's most influential newspaper.

As one might expect, the neighborhood that sprung from the farm lands owned by Granger and Jewett became a very conservative Republican stronghold for well over half a century, aiding in electing Republican North, and later Delaware District Common Councilmen, as well as Republican Mayors of Buffalo. As late as the 1950s, Parkside was a predominantly Republican district.

In the 1960's, however, the pendulum began to swing back. The election of John Kennedy to the White House, and a very likable Democrat, Frank Sedita, as Buffalo's mayor, was making it easier to win over hearts and minds all over the city.

And in 1970, Parkside joined with the rest of the Delaware Councilmatic District in electing the first Democrat ever to represent the area on Buffalo's Common Council. William B. Hoyt II was the namesake and grandson of a lawyer who worked for New York Central Railroad, was an

The home at the center of the Hoyt Mansion, shown here in the 1920s, was originally built for Buffalo's original planner Joseph Ellicott at the corner of Main and High Streets in 1828. In 1890, John Glenny moved it to Amherst Street and added on to it. William B. Hoyt purchased the home in 1910, making several additions. The Hoyt Family sold the home in the 1940s, when it was torn down to make way for the United Church Home Senior complex; which stood there until 2005, when Nichols tore the building down to make way for athletic fields.

early Pierce Arrow investor, and was integral in pulling off the 1901 Pan American Exposition in Buffalo. The elder Hoyt lived in a mansion on Amherst Street; now the site of the soccer and football fields of Nichols school.

The Younger Hoyt served on Buffalo's Common Council from 1970 until 1975, and then continued to represent the northern half of the Parkside neighborhood in the New York State Assembly from 1975 until 1992. Hoyt worked tirelessly for Parkside and the rest of his constituents, having died after suffering a heart attack on the floor of the Assembly. Since 1992, William B. Hoyt III, known to everyone as "Sam," has served in the same seat as his father in Albany. That father-son duo represents 40 years of uninterrupted elected public service for the people of Parkside.

Emblematic of the larger clash of cultures issue were the goings on at the heart of Parkside one weekend night at the height of the counter-culture movement. At the corner of Jewett Parkway and Summit Avenue, where Elam Jewett built his church "Good Shepherd," and from where the neighborhood sprung, two worlds collided.

The Frank Lloyd Wright designed Darwin Martin house had, by the late 1960s, become the official residence of the President of the University at Buffalo. Across Jewett Parkway, in the home noted Buffalo Architect William Sydney Wicks designed and built for himself, lived one of the University's most "infamous" dissident professors, Dr. Elwin H. "Ed" Powell.

Ed Powell called the house "The People's Pentagon." Powell was an early opponent of the Vietnam War, holding "teach-ins" about the conflict in 1964. He led war protests through the 60s and 70s, and sheltered war resisters at the house in 1971. His son, Jim Powell, remembers growing up in the house during that time. "The FBI and other law enforcement had the house watched for many years and the phone lines tapped. Sometimes my friends and I would go out in the middle of winter and offer the agents hot drinks while they sat there in the snow watching our house. They never accepted."

The Federal Agents also did their best to make sure the neighborhood knew of the *subversive activity* going on in their neighborhood.

"Sometimes they went door to door showing pictures of naked hippies... taken through the fence of our back yard where, at any given time during parties, there'd be dozens of naked hippies splashing around. Never a dull moment."

The photos were likely unnecessary. The younger Powell remembers his status in the neighborhood rising, as parents told their children they weren't even allowed *near* the home Jim Powell calls "a commune of Charlie Manson look-alikes with a rag-tag bunch of teenagers hanging around."

He writes of the night the UB establishment clashed with the counter culture in what he saw as "The bright shiny Cadillacs and Buicks versus the VW bugs and buses, Mavericks and Valiants."

> *The University was having a fancy party at the Frank Lloyd Wright house and invited everyone to attend the Gala Formal Event at the magnificent UB President's house at 125 Jewett Parkway on the corner of Jewett and Summit. As luck would have it, Dad was throwing a Hippie-Laden Moratorium Day blow-out party at 124 Jewett.*

> *Dad's counterculture parties at our house were legendary, yet another reason parents forbade their kids from going near the place. There were usually massive amounts of beer, often in kegs and the gallons and gallons of cheap wine flowed like the Great Niagara a few miles away. Yet that wasn't the half of it, there was so much grass and LSD, there was absolutely something for everybody. The music was amazing, the bands would set up in the large formal dining room that faced out across Jewett to the FLW house and the music was so loud it could be heard for blocks. Hundreds of people would show up for Dad's parties and by 9 PM there was usually a whole pile of hippies swimming naked in the pool.*

Dr. Powell lived in the Wicks House until his death in 2001. Before his death, Powell was able to obtain through the Freedom of Information Act, portions of his over 30,000 page FBI file. Powell's son Stephen noted in a eulogy for his father that "they had taken the great pains to go through every page and cross off the names of the informants that had contributed to this great work. Some had even lived at the house with us. He was aghast and incensed when he read the conclusion of the summary report of the file when they decided he was 'actually a pretty nice guy' and was not a terrorist threat."

Chapter 7: The Parkside Community Association

The Parkside Community Association owes its foundation in part to another group, HOME, Housing Opportunities Made Equal. According the HOME website, in 1963, *the founding members of HOME came together from a variety of racial and religious backgrounds to address the ever present problem of discrimination in the Buffalo housing market.*

The two men who founded the PCA met at a HOME meeting. "Dick Griffin and I both lived in Parkside," remembers Jack Anthony, "and met at a HOME meeting. We said HOME is good, but what about our neighborhood?

"So June, 1963, we moved my parents furniture out of their living room, we got some folding chairs from George Roberts Funeral Home, Main at Willowlawn, and we leafleted the neighborhood to say we were having a meeting about our neighborhood. We filled the living room, and a good crowd showed up. It was organized around blockbusting. So we organized, I was the first President. We had different committees. Traffic, trees. Dutch Elm Disease killing off the trees was a really big problem. A lot of people were very upset by that. We did a lot of things other than blockbusting."

But, as previously outlined, much of the group's initial effort went into preventing blockbusting. Word got out rather quickly that this wouldn't be acceptable. Early on, Parksiders decided to build an integrated community and worked for racial harmony and diversity.

"We had one black real estate agent who was accused of blockbusting. We invited him into my living room; he denied having ever done any blockbusting; and what's more, he promised he'd never do it again. That was the only real concrete incident, but the word got out-- If you trying blockbusting in Parkside, the PCA's going to be after you."

PCA wasn't just involved with keeping those that would destroy the neighborhood out; from its very beginning, the Parkside Community Association was charged with bringing new people into the neighborhood. "We distributed plenty of literature, our first pamphlet was called, *Who Needs Suburbia*. It basically said we're looking for nice neighbors no matter what color you are. So as far as most folks can see, it worked. "

David and Ruth Lampe were among the most vocal of the pioneers who helped develop the neighborhood back from its lowest point. As they were sending their children to school 54 in an effort to maintain and build upon the character of the school, the Lampes were reviving the dilapidated American Four Square they'd purchased on Crescent Avenue between Robie Street and Florence Avenue in 1970. It was one of a number of homes on the block that had seen better days.

Aside from being the PTA President at School 54, Ruth Lampe would go on to spent the next four decades as a stalwart member of the Parkside Community, acting as a block club organizer, PCA President, Housing specialist, and fighter for causes important in maintaining and growing the neighborhood.

Lampe was interviewed by the *Parkside News,* 14 years after her arrival in Parkside in 1984. "(In the mid-70s), Parkside had all the trappings of a neighborhood in trouble. Its housing stock was beginning to deteriorate; it was next to a changing community; it was relatively isolated; its local school was in trouble. Few other communities have turned around so quickly and so impressively. Parksiders can take pride in their success."

It was a major community effort, on many different levels, to make it all happen. The PCA fought against plans of The Trico Products Corporation to tear down a handful of structures along Greenfield Street near Main to build a parking lot for its plant (now the Tri-Main building). In a 1970 formal letter to city officials opposing the plan, President Richard Griffin wrote, "One primary purpose of the PCA has been to promote and retain the residential character of our community.... One city official has aptly described Trico's proposal as 'blockbusting into a residential neighborhood.'"

The PCA has also, since the early days, attempted to preserve the character of the neighborhood by insisting on strict code enforcement for both businesses and home owners.

When the PCA's Housing Committee was formed in 1967, the minutes of the Board of directors meeting said the committee should "determine what structures are (in a state of disrepair) and make efforts to persuade the owner to remedy the situation. Our purpose is not to form a vigilante committee." After identifying poorly kept premises, they worked to figure out why work wasn't being done, and helping when needed. The committee also worked to commend those who maintained their homes beautifully.

As time wore on, and despite the thought by some that the PCA should "mind its own business," the association began to take a firm stand on building codes, and encouraged the passage of codes and law which provided a legal basis to help keep the neighborhood from falling into the same condition as many other city neighborhoods. This means painting and general upkeep, but also making sure, for example, the proper permits are in place before a lawn and greenery can be cemented over and a curb cut for a parking pad.

It also applies to building usage. PCA successfully fought Buffalo State College's *Sigma Tau Rho* fraternity from opening 252 Crescent Avenue as a Frat House in 1970. UB's Dental Fraternity had operated a house at the corner of Summit and Russell Avenues for many years. The frat was described in a 1970 *Buffalo Evening News* accounting as "terrible and disastrous" for neighbors. PCA Co-Founder Dick Griffin told one reporter of "students playing loud music and cavorting on the lawn with their girlfriends. Parkside wasn't sorry to see them go."

This apartment house stood vacant, and as a collection spot for dozens of political signs until it was taken down in the early 1970s. The "Welcome to Parkside" sign now stands about where the porch is in this early 70s shot. Among the names on the political signs plastering the house: Mayor Sedita, and Common Councilmen Chester Gorski and Anthony Masiello.

The PCA also generally tries to look at preservation and rehabilitation of a property, as opposed to demolition, to prevent the blighted "gap-tooth" look seen in some city neighborhoods. One notable exception was the large apartment house which stood at the corner of Florence and Parkside Avenues in varying degrees of vacancy and vagrancy from the 1950s until the time it was torn down in the 1970s.

The Parkside Community Association was not, of course, the only community group active in Parkside. St. Vincent de Paul Roman Catholic church, which operated just south of Humboldt Parkway on Main Street for 125 years, was very much interested in the future of the city neighborhoods it served. Particularly, as a 1979 *Courier-Express* article described it, in "an aging but elegant North Buffalo apartment building. Michael Riester wrote about it in the March 2000 edition of *Parkside News:*

> *With the advent of the 1960's, St. Vincent's bravely confronted the great social changes underway. Under the direction of Msgr. Paul Valente, parishioners turned their attention to concerns facing her neighborhood. St. Vincent's joined the fight to oppose redlining, the illegal banking practice of refusing to loan money for inner city home purchases. Describing the changing mission of the traditional parish, Msgr. Valente is quoted as saying, "What it's becoming is more of a community center. We are trying to become more community conscious and les missionary in the old sense of going out to make converts. We simply want to indicate by our concern and action that we feel a part of the community, and that we have the interests of the community at heart.*

> *Encouraged by Msgr. Valente, an enthusiastic group of parishioners became a part of the Community Action Organization. This grassroots organization involved 16 catholic parishes who decide to try to fight redlining by peaceful means... During the summer of 1975, a group of parishioners began an in-depth study of slumlords within the (Parkside) neighborhood. They focused their attention on the owner of the Crescent Apartments at 196 Crescent Avenue. Having gained the support of the tenants, committee members actually accompanied city housing inspectors through each apartment, making a list of needed repairs. At one point, over seventy-five neighbors demanded a meting with Mayor Makowski and city housing inspectors to address a list of over seventy-five code violations within the building. A meeting did take place at the St. Vincent's Parish rectory, and through repeated exposure in the Buffalo News, the building was sold to a new owner.*

Ruth Lampe has been a stickler for housing and building code compliance, and has served as the PCA's Housing Specialist. In a 1984 interview about housing, Lampe said, "PCA's controversial and largely successful housing program ensured that the area's housing stock was well maintained, even in cases where owners would not have otherwise afforded to make improvements. We often take this community for granted. We need to have some historical perspective. (In 1974), housing prices were depressed and we had real problems. Now (in 1984), while everything is not perfect, we have solved the number one problem-- the stability and attractiveness of the community. "

94 Jewett Parkway stands as a testament to mixed use in Parkside. A state-run group home site since 1986, the home was designed by well regarded Buffalo firm Esenwein and Johnson, and built by Mr. Sinclair, who made millions in the millinery business; making the ornate sort of women's hats that were in style in the 1890s. The last private owner of the home was very intrigued about a large walk-in vault below the back porch, so he paid a locksmith rather handsomely to open the obviously long locked safe. There was great suspense as the door creaked open, with hopes of some long-forgotten riches. Suspense turned to great hope as there was, to everyone's surprise... a single box in the safe. The box was excitedly cracked open to find... A stash of girlie magazines.

Parkside's efforts to "Preserve a Neighborly Neighborhood" became the title of an article published in *The National Observer*, in 1972, which acted as a weekend edition for the Wall Street Journal. PCA Co-founder Richard

Griffin takes a reporter on a tour of the neighborhood which had just undergone a decade of momentous change. The mood of the piece is, *we're hopeful, working on it, and hoping for the best.*

The hoping and the work paid off. "Parkside inspires more confidence than it did four or five years ago. One real estate broker confided that one of the reasons for the Elmwood-Delaware Area's resurgence was the number of people fearful of investing in Parkside," Real Estate Reporter Phillip Langdon wrote in a 1979 *Buffalo Evening News* larger piece on the "comeback" of the city as a whole. The article continued:

> *(Richard) Mabee (of Gurney, Becker, and Bourne Realty) confirms what Parkside residents say -- that "Parkside has gained a lot of appeal. It's become a very successful integrated neighborhood."*

> *Some nervous whites moved out, but Mabee says "those spots were filled in not only by successful blacks but by university people, who are more broadminded."..."They're active and they're smart," Mabee says of (the Parkside Community Association).*

A 1977 Parkside newsletter quotes a Community Planning Assistance Center (CPAC) study of the changes in Parkside, comparing the area in 1970 to the way it was in 1977.

> *The Parkside community residential housing prices have increased on average from $21,500 to $33,500 in 1977. The sales listings have decreased from a 1973 high of 92 to a 1976 total of 46, which can be interpreted as a sign of confidence in the area as viewed by its residents.... Owner occupied dwellings have increased from 895 in 1970 to 925 in 1975, an increase of 30 units.*

The same 1977 newsletter came with a page labeled "Thoughts on Our Neighborhood," a sample of opinions offered up by members:

> *We have young children, young married couples, old married couples, retirees, grandparents, blacks, whites, others, blue collars, white collars, laborers, professionals, liberals, conservatives, moderates, radicals, reactionaries, anarchists, entrepreneurs, communists, all living together... one from many.*

Many opinions also focused on the slowly upgrading housing stock, and the varied nature of the areas homes, and a still tempered hope for the future of the neighborhood.

The PCA would take a major role in bolstering those tempered hopes, but only with the active support of the people of the neighborhood. It was still a topic of great interest when written about in the February 1981 *Parkside News*:

> *Although you might not be aware of it, the 'renaissance' of the Parkside community has taken a lot of work by your neighbors over the past few years. Building code enforcement, tree planting, zoning enforcement, solving small community problems, and housing improvements have been among the main concerns of the Association.*
>
> *As the Parkside Community Association has progressed, the resident involvement it has stimulated has been the major force in the perception and creative dealing with newly emerging neighborhood needs. Three years ago, in 1977, in response to the perception that the neighborhood was in need of a defined preservation and restoration program, the membership voted to open a formal office with the assistance of outside funding. PCA was awarded community development funds to help with its programs. In 1979, New York State Division of Housing and Community Renewal funds were added to the PCA's budget.*

Despite all the successes, challenges continued. While blockbusting was corralled very early on, redlining has lasted in various forms even up to this day, and the fact that it is so institutionalized, makes it very difficult to fight. When the term first came into usage, it referenced the practice of denying loans and insurance (or allowing loans or insurance but at incredibly raised rates) to people in communities that banks and insurance companies found undesirable (usually that meant poor or black.) The definition expanded to include other businesses that would deny basic services or adequate access to services based on geographic location.

The Community Association's annual spring meeting in 1976 was entitled, "Redlining and Disinvestment. The Erie County Citizens Organization present their findings of 'banking disinvestment' in Buffalo." Finding loans to buy or renovate a home in the area was getting increasing difficult, as was finding reasonably priced home owners insurance for many.

Other societal changes made some other forms of redlining more apparent as well. Up until the mid '70s, a family's groceries could, for the most part, be purchased within the confines of Parkside. Grocers like Red & White would have fruits and canned goods, one of the several delicatessens had smaller items. At various times there were butchers and bakers. But with the rise of supermarkets, came the fall of the Mom and Pop stores, and residents had to rely on the behemoth stores outside of the neighborhood confines for groceries.

Main & West Oakwood, across Oakwood from Parkside Candy, 1950s

By the early 80s, many were beginning to question the variety at the area markets. Most Parksiders shopped at The Bells in Central Park Plaza, The Super Duper on Great Arrow near Delaware, and the Tops on Delaware at Linden. It was observed that the fresh meats and produce weren't as fresh or plentiful as in suburban stores, and that some staple items, like milk and bread, were priced higher for city shoppers.

Taking it on as an obvious quality of life issue, The PCA publicly campaigned for changes. The manager of each store was called out in editorials in the *Parkside News* and in the larger press, and it was insisted that such practices wouldn't be tolerated. It's just a small example of raising the quality of life in many different ways to make the area more attractive to people willing and able to invest.

Throughout the 1970s, one major investment Parksiders looked forward to was the building of the *LRRT,* light rail rapid transit, right along

Parkside's spine on Main Street. For over a decade, residents actively participated in deciding where the stops should be placed in the neighborhood. By the time the *MetroRail* plans were set in 1982, it was thought 10,000 people a day would be arriving and departing from the Amherst Street station every day. Many Parksiders (and City Planners) of the day saw this as the future of the neighborhood. All around the country, areas newly serviced by light rail had always seen property values escalate.

While in retrospect, the projected numbers fell way short of expectation, and the project wasn't the panacea that many thought it might be, it still helped give Parkside a boost.

The June 1981 *Parkside News* headline read, *Housing Values in Parkside Soar.* Just as average home value increased and the number of sales dropped 1970-77, 1979-81 saw more stabilization, based in part of the impending opening of the *MetroRail*. The 1979 MLS average for homes sold in Parkside was $27,800. A year later, it had jumped to $35,800. There were also 50% fewer sales. Area home values increased 28.5% 1979 to 1980, as compared to an only 8.3% increase in WNY as a whole.

In 1984, UB's Department of Environmental Design conducted an analysis of the Parkside neighborhood, looking to see how the Comprehensive Code Enforcement program affected the community. As far as housing values, they rose 29% in Buffalo between 1978 and 1982. In Parkside, housing values rose 56% during the same period.

With the future of the neighborhood on a much more firm footing by the mid 1980s, many stopped worrying about treading water, and began looking to the future. Many looked at the past as a means to ensure the future. By 1983, an initial survey of the Parkside neighborhood was completed by *the Friends of Olmsted Parks*, with the hope and expectation that the Olmsted-designed neighborhood might be recognized on the National Register of Historic Places.

Over the next few years, a complete survey was completed, with the efforts spearheaded by Erie County Legislator Joan Bozer, she a Parkside resident. The full document is over 1,000 pages, and includes a two page summary of every building within Parkside, and painstakingly inventories the historic relevance of every article of the neighborhood's landscape:

The Parkside... Historic District in Buffalo, New York is located
approximately four miles north of Buffalo's central business district at the

east and northeast sides of Delaware Park. The district is characterized by an irregular street pattern, which generally follows the contours of the adjacent park's edge, and by a large number of single family residences built for middle and upper-middle class families during the nineteenth and early twentieth centuries.

The Parkside... Historic District covers a relatively flat, crescent-shaped area of approximately 226 acres. There are 1768 contributing buildings included in the district; 1109 represent principal buildings and 659 are outbuildings, usually garages. Three of the contributing buildings were listed on the National Register in 1975 as part of the Darwin Martin House Complex... The district also includes nine contributing structures, representing historic streets and street segments significant for their association with Frederick Law Olmsted's 1876 and c.1886 plans for the development of "Parkside." These features comprise: Agassiz Circle, Amherst Street, Crescent Avenue, Greenfield Street, Humboldt Parkway, Jewett Parkway, Parkside Avenue, Summit Avenue, and Woodward Avenue. There are 22 non-contributing principal buildings in the historic district. Most of these are infill housing units or post-1926 apartment buildings; however, several represent severely altered buildings constructed within the district's 1876-1936 period of significance.

In 1987, Parkside officially won the Historic Designation. PCA Board President Robert A. Kilduff wrote about it in the *Parkside News*:

The real benefit of the designation is more intangible, more psychological than financial. It involves recognition of the value of what we have inherited as well as a renewed commitment to preserve it....

The Historic designation has also seen an increase in activism in the affairs of the Park. Parkside was designed around the Park, and was seen by Olmsted as an integral part of the Park System. Parkside was created as a built-in protector of the Park system, serving to buffer the Park from inappropriate uses. Now, many Parksiders complain that Delaware Park is no longer seen as a part of the community by "the powers that be," but as a regional entity... PCA's watch dogging of conditions an usage of the park has seemed parochial to some, but the mission of Parkside is more than parochialism, but rather an historic mission.

That same year was watershed year for the Community Association, as in March 1987, a PCA was established with the purchase of a new headquarters building. The PCA committed to buy and renovate the former dental offices of Dr. Monreith Hollway at 2318 Main Street, which included the office as well as two units of low income housing. Initial renovation costs, to be provided by two state grants, were to total $71,000. "Owning the building is seen by PCA as a commitment to renovating a visible and deteriorating community resource."

2318 Main Street was slated for demolition before it was purchased and renovated by the Parkside Community Association. 1987 photo.

But it wasn't as easy as initially thought. By January, 1990, difficult and costly renovations had dragged on, and the PCA was being evicted from its previous office space at 10 W Oakwood Place, as owner was trying to sell the building. The PCA had lost state funding to refurbish the building at 2318 Main Street, and the project was becoming entangled in a web of city, state, and federal regulations.

But the many problems were overcome, and, by mid 1991, as the PCA got ready to move into its building at 2318 & 2320 Main Street, one longtime Parkside Resident was awash with memories. Milton Carlin remembered his father's jewelry store was on the right side of the two store-front building. At that time, the left side was Russell's Barber Shop, At that point, the building's dentist owner, Dr. Hollway, practiced upstairs. The jewelry store existed in the space through the 1940s, when Dr. Hollway moved his practice into the storefront. It remains today the PCA headquarters.

The offices of Dr. Monreith Hollway; now the PCA Office, 2318 Main Street

As the neighborhood and the focus of the community association changed, one man greatly credited with keeping neighbors on track was Derek Bateman; the Executive Director of PCA from 1982-1992. As he left, he was lauded as greatly responsible for helping to turn around the attitudes about the neighborhood's housing stock. "He saw the neighborhood through its comprehensive code enforcement, a process that upset many homeowners, but brought about dramatic changes in the physical appearance of the area."

Bateman wrote at the end of his tenure that plenty of what was seen and *what was not seen* in Parkside had been influenced by the PCA during his time as Executive Director:

> There are no video arcades at the corner of Main and Amherst or Parkside and Russell, and nor are there disruptive bars at Parkside and Russell. There is a stoplight at the intersection of Florence and Parkside, and many new trees along Parkside's streets.

There is a newly renovated Parkside-Florence tot lot, initiated by interested residents working with the PCA. The new historic street lights, now being put up, would have been inappropriate suburban looking fixtures had it not been for PCA intervention.

While neighborhoods around the city continued to deteriorate, Parkside, with its strong community, and strong community association prospered. But maybe too much, as a double edged sword came for the PCA in 1996: The State of New York's Department of Housing and Community Renewal determined that the Parkside Community Association met its original goal of creating a stable and economically diverse neighborhood.

While this milestone came as great news, it also came with the state ending its yearly grant of $63,000, nearly immediately, as of March 1996. It came as a shock, and caused the organization to change the way it had operated for many years. Three jobs, and one proposed job, were eliminated from the PCA. The organization had long been open for housing assistance for low income homeowners. Those requests were being forwarded to the North Buffalo Community Center. New emphasis was put on membership and fundraising. The writing of grants and annual requests of city, county and state lawmakers became yearly events.

Keeping a Thumb on City Living Constants

While maintaining the value and physical appearance of housing stock is of critical importance, so too, were a number of other battles the PCA has fought along the way. The Parkside Community Association has led many charges over the years in keeping the community one of the city's most envied, as "Parkside's voice" as the city evolved.

As Buffalo hemorrhaged population, and the city made infrastructure changes and consolidations, Parksiders and the PCA fought to maintain a fair share. When Buffalo's neighborhood Police precincts gave way to the plan dividing the city into 5 much larger districts, PCA was there making sure that Police protection wouldn't drop off when the Precinct 17 House at Colvin and Linden was closed in favor of the D District house on Hertel Avenue.

The PCA was also there a decade earlier in 1982 as Councilmatic districts were re-drawn, with one proposal cutting Parkside in half. This plan was quickly abandoned by city planners with the voices of Parksiders heard.

The Association also played a major role in the development of School 54 first into a Center of Excellence School, and then as an Early Childhood Learning Center, riding the changes of the Buffalo Public Schools over the last several decades. Through the 1970s and 80s, the PCA went after funds to help in a defined preservation and restoration program for the homes of the community and the neighborhood at large. Ruth Lampe, once the PTA President at 54 has taken great pride in the positive change at the school saying, "the magnet school concept and Buffalo's successful desegregation efforts made the community more attractive because families moving to Parkside could choose from a range of options."

Traffic

Since the building of the Scajaquada and Kensington Expressways in the 1950s and 1960s, the streets of Parkside have become heavily traveled by the people of North Buffalo, Kenmore, and Tonawanda as the quickest way to get to the expressways to get downtown or to get back home.

Among the early proposed solutions to congestion, a 1965 investigation into the feasibility of an underpass where Parkside Avenue and the Scajaquada Expressway meet. It was the first of many times the community would become involved in traffic patterns in the neighborhood. It was the work of people living in the neighborhoods that brought 4-way stop signs, and all of the traffic signals along Parkside Avenue to the area as traffic calming measures.

The first block of Russell became one way at the request of residents; the traffic signal at Parkside and Russell Avenues was added at the behest of residents and the zoo in 1987.

A decade earlier, it was a much more intense battle for the traffic light at Parkside and Florence Avenues. Even after deaths occurred in traffic accidents at the dangerous curve and intersection, it took years of fighting to have the device finally erected.

Residents argued that the signal wasn't just necessary for drivers, but for pedestrians looking to get into the park. In 1976, the light was deemed unnecessary by the City Commissioner of Transportation Daniel Hoyt, despite that sharp curve and the numerous reports of damage to trees and homes at the intersection as motorists left the road.

A compromise was agreed upon with Commissioner Hoyt, as he

promised to erect a traffic light at Parkside and Florence Avenues if neighbors agreed to allow a playground on park land near the intersection. $23,000 in block grants built the tot lot, which stands today; very near the still standing traffic light.

The Parkside Bar Scene

Like most city neighborhoods, traffic wasn't the worst of it. At one point in the not too distant past, a handful of bars and taverns dotted the Parkside neighborhood, especially on Main Street and Parkside Avenue.

The PCA investigated and wrote letters on behalf of neighbors near the Casa Savoy Bar at Main Street and Orchard Place in 1968. In the late 1980s, neighbors and the PCA fought against efforts to turn the former Parkside Candy Shoppe at Main Street and West Oakwood Place into a bar. The Parkside *Sweet* Shoppe was open for several months selling desserts and booze, but didn't last.

However, since the advent of the Parkside Community Association, there has been no one single business to receive more complaints, from more neighbors, than the Park Meadow Restaurant.   Located at the corner of Parkside and Russell Avenues, *The PM* was originally a restaurant where many parishioners of St Marks and St Vincents grabbed their Friday fish fry, and left the neighborhood swathed in the inviting classic Buffalo smells of grease-soaked beer batter.

All during the 60s and 70s, the Park Meadow was a big hangout for Canisius College students, as well as several area high schools. At night it would get pretty rowdy, lots of beer drinking; not illegal activity per se, just a public nuisance for the folks right around the bar. In the mid 70s, Dennis Brinkworth purchased the property, removed the kitchen, put in a full bar, and the problems amplified. Neighbors had more complaints about drunken youths, tossing beer cups and tossing their cookies onto lawns for blocks around the gin mill.

Neighbors and the PCA viewed Brinkworth as hostile towards their concerns. Brinkworth always claimed he was just trying to run a business. Before the conversion to a full bar, Brinkworth said he "was lucky to make $40 a night and practically had to give away the fish fry."

In 1979, three young men who'd been drinking all night at the Park Meadow, broke into the zoo and began attacking the polar bears, throwing large stones and trash cans into their pit. One of the young men was injured as, in a drunken stupor; he fell into that bear pit. This and other incidents lead to the eventual revocation of the bar's liquor license. The PCA has fought numerous attempts since to sell alcohol at the building, and has let subsequent restaurant managers know from the outset, that the community wouldn't support the sale of any spirituous beverage on the premises.

The experience also hardened PCA activists to other business in the neighborhood as well, making sure that business plans, and plans for keeping the peace were clearly spelled out. In 1983, neighbors fought an attempt by one-time Buffalo State basketball star and Buffalo Braves great Randy Smith from opening a video arcade on Main Street near the corner of Vernon at 2612 Main. The Common Council twice rejected a bid for license from the on-time NBA iron man because of concerns the *Buffalo News* reported as potential "loitering and minor crimes."

Violent Crime

While Parkside has dealt with petty crime just as any other city neighborhood has, violent crime - even random murder - has also scarred the neighborhood on rare occasions. In 1961, Delaware Park took on a very sinister feel. Young Andrew Ashly was kidnapped from his family's Jewett Parkway home, his body later found in the artificial lake in the quarry behind the Lodge (at Parkside and Florence Avenues) in the park.

Some remember a liquor store owner was murdered inside his

Parkside store in a holdup in the early 1970s, and around the same time, three teens were stabbed in an apparently racially motivated attack near Main Street and West Oakwood Place.

In the early to mid 1980s, a string of rapes occurred in and around the Delaware Park area, close to the *David* statue. A West Side man, Anthony Capozzi was convicted for several of the attacks. However, it was only two decades later that a task force convened to catch a serial killer collared the actual Delaware Park Rapist. Through DNA analysis and the man's own admission of guilt, these rapes were properly connected to the man who had become known as the Bike Path Rapist and Bike Path Killer, Altemio Sanchez. Capozzi, who bore a striking resemblance to Sanchez at the time, was exonerated and set free from prison.

Greenfield Street was rocked both literally and figuratively when, in 1987, an explosion and fire gutted the 46 Greenfield Street home of Gerard Ciccarelli. This, the fourth arson at the home, coincided with the day Ciccarelli was to be released from prison after serving a year for luring a 16 year old Cheektowaga girl to his home and molesting her.

Though Judge John Dillon denounced Ciccarelli as a "reprehensible lecher" who'd been arrested 14 times on 35 charges, neighbors told the *Buffalo News* at the time of the fire that they "resent the implication that anyone in the neighborhood was involved in anyway."

Unfortunately, homicide isn't foreign to the area, either. In 1984, 89 year old Alma Strasner was raped and viciously beaten to death at her Willowlawn Avenue home. The case went unsolved for 24 years, until 2008, when Buffalo Police Cold Case Detectives ran evidence from the scene through the national DNA databank. They came up with a hit. Edward Richardson, who was in jail in Seattle on misdemeanor charges, was once a handyman who had done work for and lived on Crescent Avenue, around the corner from Mrs. Strasner. Erie County District Attorney Frank J. Clark credited Detectives Charles Aronica and Mary Gugliazza with reopening the investigation and submitting blood evidence for a DNA analysis. Richardson eventually pleaded guilty to second degree murder and was sentenced to 18 years to life in prison.

More recently, on Good Friday 2006, 41 year old George Pitiliangas was gunned down as he closed up his 2285 Main St. Restaurant. The long-time owner of Tony's Ranch House was closing up the popular Parkside eatery, was once home to Henry's Hamburgers, when 23 year old Amhir

Cole gunned him down in the store. Cole is serving life without parole, plus 25 years. Judge Michael D'Amico leveled the unusually heavy sentence after Cole had convinced a mentally challenged man to admit to the murder.

A memorial for Pitiliangas in the restaurant's parking lot drew hundreds from Parkside, Central Park, and the Fillmore/Leroy neighborhoods, with more than one observer commenting that George's tragic death brought folks from all walks of life, and both sides of Main Street together, just as his restaurant did. Pitiliangas' mother reopened the restaurant 45 days after the shooting.

Parkside's Houses of Worship Today

After 129 years on the same block of Main Street, Parkside's first church, St. Vincent de Paul was closed. In 1992, the Catholic Diocese of Buffalo began announcing plans to reduce the number of parishes on the

St. Vincent's was known for it's Latin mass, seen here in 1992, Fr. Valentine Welker officiating.

Central East Side of Main Street from ten to five. Despite consternation and the heavy hearts of many in the financially sound parish, St. Vincent's was merged with Blessed Trinity, several blocks away on Leroy Street. The buildings of St. Vincent de Paul were sold by the Diocese to Canisius College for $250,000. Many St. Vincent's parishioners harbor a deep anger and resentment about the process to this day.

At the final mass on the Feast of Pentecost, May 30, 1993, a remembrance booklet was handed out to parishioners. It's fitting closing quote, as noted by Michael Riester, "the physical structure may not last forever, but the love and spirit of St. Vincent's will live on in us... These things of God indeed do not perish." The prayers of many Parkside residents were answered when the church was not torn down, but given a $3.4 million face lift and opened as the 515-seat Montante Cultural Center in October, 2000.

The closure of St. Vincent de Paul leaves St. Marks as the neighborhood's lone Catholic church. Msgr. Francis Braun and Sr. Jeanne

Eberle have spent more than 25 years at the helm of St. Mark Church and School. Dubbed the "Dynamic Duo" of St. Mark's by Bishop Edward Kmiec, he awarded them *The 2009 Bishops Medal* for 60 combined years of faithful and dedicated service to the parish. Both have lent their names to buildings on the St Mark campus. In 2004, as the community celebrated his 24th anniversary of service to St. Mark's, his Golden Jubilee as a priest, and his 75th birthday, The *Rev. Francis Braun Auditorium* was dedicated. Upon completion of improvements at the school in June 2008, the lower level classroom wing was named The *Sr. Jeanne Eberle SSJ Wing of Academic Excellence.*

Upon receiving the area-wide recognition of the Bishop's award, neither Msgr. Braun nor Sr. Jeanne wanted to speak about themselves, but did want to talk about the school and the community. "We want to feature the school," Msgr. Braun told the *WNY Catholic*. "People in North Buffalo already know about it, but (the award) is a means of letting the rest of the city know about the school."

"Father (Braun) is very interested in the school, which is great," said Sister Jeanne. "He boosts the school all the time."

"Because it's good for the neighborhood," added Msgr. Braun. The school has been good for the neighborhood, and vice versa. While many parish schools closed through the 90s and 00s, people moved to Parkside because of St Mark's School, and St. Mark's School stayed open and healthy because of the health and vitality of the neighborhood.

Over the years, many have made comments about the pair working together for so long, a rarity in this day and age, that one of them, let alone both, would stay in the same post for so long. "They said it's like being married," joked Msgr. Braun. "I said, 'No, no. We send notes to one another and see each other every few weeks.' And they said, 'That's like being married!'"

The Episcopal Church of the Good Shepherd continues on as well; searching for a rector at the time of publication. Whoever takes the job will be filling the large shoes of Rev. David Selzer, who was at Good Shepherd for over 13 years. Selzer always made sure that his church was part of the larger community, and vice versa. "In the same way the founders of this church, as a memorial chapel to Rev. Ingersoll of Trinity Church in Downtown Buffalo, envisioned both a church and a community center, we are continuing that tradition of being a presence in the Parkside Community.

We obviously do worship, and are a part of that sense of a worshipping community, but were also doing outreach in terms of community service. AA meetings, dog obedience classes, ballet classes, PCA meetings, planned parenthood meetings, being the home base for the Parkside Home Tour, any number of activities in which the community is involved.

"Part of the result is you have people who see themselves as members here by virtue of their worship, but there are also people who are members by participating in any one of those activities. At the same time, there's the outreach function of this congregation. We've had a viable food pantry for the past 15 years, on Monday morning, a lot of folks who see people coming and say, 'They don't look like Parkside people,' but they see themselves as a part of the community because they receive food.

"Church is both a place to worship, and a place to be a part of. The Halloween Party has been here 25 years plus. So now we have parents, who came here for Halloween bringing their kids here. This is *their Halloween* party. It doesn't belong to the church or the Parkside Community Association. It's a place to be safe, and place to get treats that they know won't have something awful in them, and it's also a place where the fire department, and the police department can bring canines and do their stuff with the kids as well. "

Just up Jewett Parkway, Central Presbyterian had been experiencing a steady decline in membership for years. At its height, there were over 3,000 members at Central. By 1985, membership had shrunk to about 800; by the mid-2000's, it was in double digits. The huge costs of maintaining the buildings overwhelmed the congregation's ability to support them, and a buyer was sought for the whole  campus. After two years of leasing its buildings to a charter school, the grounds were sold to Mt. St. Joseph Academy in 2007. In May 2008, the 30 members of Central Presbyterian officially merged with First Presbyterian

Church. Ironically, it was approximately the same number, roughly thirty, that left First Presbyterian over 170 years earlier to form Central.

Since 1971, just outside the boundaries of Parkside, at the corner of Amherst Street and Parker Street, stands *Masjid Taqwa,* a mosque owned by The Islamic Society of Niagara Frontier. While still maintaining the Parker Street building, An-Noor Masjid was built established in Amherst 1995 and is one of the largest Masjids (the Arabic word for mosque) in Western New York. Currently, ISNF is supervising the complete renovation of the interior of the Parker Street Masjid.

After having spent most of the last half century as a funeral home, Parkside's oldest home, The Washington Adams Russell house, is now the home of *The Church in Buffalo.* On its website, *The Church* writes," We are Christians who frequently meet together at 2540 Main Street in Buffalo, as well as in our homes. The building in which we meet on Main Street is our meeting hall; it is not *the church.* We, the believers in Christ, are *the church.* The word *church* in the original language of the Bible, and in its true meaning, simply stands for the believers themselves, the *called-out congregation.* We are not any special kind or *group* of Christians, but simply those who believe in and love the Lord Jesus and meet together in one accord with gladness and singleness of heart (Acts 2:46). We do not really have a name, although some have tried to give us one. We are simply believers in Jesus Christ who desire only to hold and honor the precious Name of our Lord Jesus. In the first century, believers were simply *Christians* (1 Peter 4:16), and that was a name given to them by others (Acts 11:26)."

Refreshing Springs Church is in the building that was built as the Park Presbyterian Church on Elam Place, between Crescent Avenue and Jewett Parkway, in 1897. Refreshing Springs vision is "Helping men, women and families from multiple economic and ethnic backgrounds to truly know Jesus, making disciples throughout W.N.Y. , and the world, through evangelism, planting churches, equipping workers, and establishing leaders."

Institutions of Learning

Aside from bringing a certain air to the neighborhood, the many institutions of learning in Parkside, including two of the three largest private colleges in the area, have also brought many real, tangible positives to Parkside as well.

Canisius College actually financially encourages its employees to live in Parkside. Its Employer Assisted Housing Program began in 2002, and faculty and staff can receive up to $7000 for buying a home in Parkside or another eligible city neighborhood.

But even more tangible, Canisius, as well as the other neighborhood schools, have been at the forefront of reusing buildings that, in other parts of the city, might have gone abandoned. Since the mid-80s, Canisius College has grown from 12 acres to 30 acres, with much of that growth in Parkside.

Indeed, Canisius has purchased and invested millions of dollars in many buildings mentioned in this narrative. In Parkside, the college purchased the former Streng Oldsmobile Dealership. The former Sears Store, more recently the Western New York Headquarters for Blue Cross/Blue Shield is now the Canisius Science center. All of the buildings that were once a part of the St. Vincent de Paul parish are all now Canisius buildings. Many of the Sisters of St. Joseph buildings on the west side of Main Street have been sold to Canisius, including, the most recent home of Mount St. Joseph Academy, which has been raised by Canisius to make way for future development.

It's caused somewhat of a domino effect, with Mount St Joseph's Academy then moving into the former Central Presbyterian church at Main and Jewett. No longer directly affiliated with the Sisters, the students of Mount St. Joe's Elementary enjoy a 7:1 student to teacher ratio.

At the heart of the Buffalo area's third largest private college is another former Mount St Joseph's structure. The main building at Medaille was until the mid-80s, the home of Mount St Joseph High School. Medaille saw a 138% increase in enrollment 1995-2003, and its over three thousand students ranks the school just behind neighboring Canisius and Niagara in size. Medaille owns many of the beautiful homes on Humboldt Parkway near the school.

Another institution started by the Sisters of St. Joseph still going strong in Parkside is St. Mary's School for the Deaf. *SMSD* carries on the traditions brought to the corner of Main Street and Dewey Avenue over 110 years ago. The school's efforts to reach out to the neighboring communities continue with plans for a student-run coffee house in Parkside. Hoping to capitalize on the explosive popularity of the Darwin Martin House, plans to open The *Elam Jewett Café* in Jewett Hall at the Church of the Good Shepherd continue to progress.

While not an educational institution, the Tri-Main Center is perhaps the area's most creative re-use of a building. A year after Trico abandoned its factory at Main Street and Rodney Avenue, in 1988, Tri-Main began offering its mixed-use office, studio and light industrial facilities.

But whatever you call *Tri-Main*, don't call it a plant. Matt Wolfe has helped market the complex over the years, and told *Business First* in 2002, "It's funny because if you can get them away from thinking of this place as a factory, most people walk around here and say 'Geez, I didn't know all this was here'," Wolfe said. "Besides, I guess by calling it the 'old Trico plant', it does give them a point of reference and an idea of where we are."

Tri-Main is also Parkside's best link to the current White House. Kittinger manufactures its fine furniture at its Tri-Main factory and workshop. In the same space where Ford Model-Ts and America's first jet plane were manufactured, Kittinger artisans design and build furniture for the White House, including the "fireside chairs" both Presidents Barack Obama and George W. Bush sat in during their inaugural ceremonies.

Parkside Goes Hollywood

Though usually thought of in terms of a staid, august, and venerable neighborhood, Parkside has also seen its share of glitz and glamour. For the same reason so many Buffalonians are attracted to its wonderful architecture and tree-lined streets, Hollywood producers have also taken notice over the years.

For three weeks in February, 1982, Summit Avenue went Hollywood for a week. Burt Reynolds and Goldie Hawn spent that time holed up at 45 Summit Avenue, shooting scenes for the big screen motion picture *Best Friends*. The local accommodations were much cheaper than the LA high rollers were used to, as Ellen Parisi wrote in her History of the Good Shepherd Church, only a few doors down from the home where most of the film was shot:

In order to accommodate the cast's and crew's noon meal, the advance people made arrangements to rent Jewett Memorial Hall. "Probably the biggest mistake I ever made," said Fr. Jerre Feagin, Good Shepherd rector 1978-82, "was not charging them more. When they asked how much it would cost to rent the hall for three weeks, I said, 'One Thousand dollars.' that was a lot of money to the Church of the Good Shepherd. But the man looked at me with great surprise in his eyes, as if to say, 'Is that all?' and he immediately wrote a check."

Production trucks for BEST FRIENDS line up along Summit Avenue

The Parkside home of Alex Trammell and the Buffalo snow provided the perfect backdrop for producers. Signs outside of the home pleaded for untracked snow... But one four-legged critter didn't see the sign and spoiled the scene producers had hoped for, namely virgin, freshly fallen snow. But that errant dog didn't provide the only challenge to filming:

"There was one problem with a neighbor who didn't want (the film people) there," Fr. Feagin continued. "It was a nuisance. They roped the streets off. Mounted police were all over keeping intruders out. Big sound and power

trucks came in at 5am and parked all over the streets. There were catering trucks selling things. It was like a carnival. Well, this one neighbor didn't like it, and in protest, every time they'd begin filming, he'd run his lawnmower. In February. The director, Norman Jewison, approached me and asked me to do something. The man causing the trouble was a Roman Catholic, so I called Fr. Braun from St. Mark's and he straightened it out. That movie company was only a few hours from packing up and leaving town in search of a new location if Fr. Braun hadn't been able to stop the noise."

Above: from The Natural. Glenn Close and Robert Redford on Main St at W Oakwood Pl. Below: Redford standing in roughly the same location, from a different angle.

Hollywood was back in Parkside the following year, this time at the corner of Main Street and West Oakwood Place for the shooting of *The Natural*. Glenn Close and Robert Redford spent a few days in August, 1983 at the Parkside Candy Shoppe. The no-nonsense long time owners of the ice cream parlor, Ted and Sandy Malamas, told the *Parkside News* in 1988 that they were impressed with Close, who garnered an Academy Award Nomination for her role in the film. Given their silence on the rest of the cast, *one can draw ones own conclusion.*

The scenes shot inside the store were, according to the story, taking place in Chicago. A large matrix of I-beams was erected of Main Street at Oakwood to give the appearance of Chicago's elevated train. Filming of the movie also took place at War Memorial Stadium and All-High Stadium, the Buffalo Schools field just up the street behind Bennett High School.

After a twenty year hiatus from *Tinsletown*, Parkside returned to the small screen in 2003 as the setting for the MTV Reality Series *Sorority Life*. Season 2 of the show featured the Delta Xi Omega sorority from the University at Buffalo. Their sorority house for 2002 was at the southwest corner of Crescent and West Oakwood. Shooting for the show happened all over the neighborhood, but perhaps most publicly at Kostas Restaurant on Hertel Avenue, where cameras followed one of the sisters to work as a waitress.

Parkside also played a dark role in a similar MTV show shot in Buffalo the following year. Three UB students were arrested after breaking into the Buffalo Zoo in 2003 as a part of a videotaped stunt for the show *Fraternity Life*. In an incident reminiscent of stunts dreamt up after a night of collegiate drinking at the Park Meadow two decades earlier, The pledges were to break into to the zoo, and take an animal home as a pet.

Parkside's Biggest Battle: The Buffalo Zoo

For better or for worse, the histories of Parkside and the Buffalo Zoological Gardens have really been inseparable. From Elam Jewett's care of the first two deer donated to the city in 1870, to the arrival of Frank the Elephant in 1905, to the Depression-era WPA improvements that built the Zoo up and out, to the fight to keep the Zoo at Delaware Park, the Buffalo Zoo and Parkside have seen their fates intertwined since either has existed.

At the Zoo, Buffalo, N. Y.

By 1930, however, the zoo had seriously deteriorated. Nearly 20 years had passed since any improvements were funded by the city. Indignant citizens carried on letter campaigns to the newspapers and City

Hall. The animals and the site had been suffering severe neglect. In 1931, the Zoological Society was organized, but the throes of the Great Depression made it impossible to raise money to improve the zoo.

It would take the New Deal programs of President Franklin Roosevelt to refurbish the Zoo. Starting in 1935, $1.5 million dollars worth of federal WPA money was poured into a structural modernization project. Many murals and stone sculptures *(left, 1946)* were added to the grounds, and a gleaming new building was opened by 1938, but it was largely empty for lack of funding for new specimens.

That changed under the directorship of Marlin Perkins. Later famous as the host of Mutual of Omaha's Wild Kingdom from 1958- 1985, while in Buffalo, Perkins grew the popularity of the zoo, particularly through the training of some animals, like Eddie the Chimp, to perform for the crowds. Another $840,000 in WPA funds allowed for more work in 1939, and in 1942, the reptile house was opened. Perkins left in a wage dispute in 1944.

Marlin Perkins (right) and Fred Meyer 1941, Zoo Photo

Still woefully under funded, the zoo installed concession

stands and a train ride around the zoo in 1950 to help raise money for improvements. Cries about litter and a carnival-like atmosphere grew even louder when 21 people were injured when the miniature train toppled over in 1952. To encourage people to drive to the zoo, The *Parkside-Quarried Limestone* Farmstead home was razed in 1950 to provide parking for the zoo. *(see photo page 36)*

Things had only gotten worse for the zoo, when, upon a tour of the facility in 1958, Mayor Frank Sedita declared Buffalo should either have a zoo *to be proud of,* or none at all. The grounds were closed to the public for 5 months, and $300,000 was spent in renovations. The new and improved zoo was opened to the public in March 1959. And despite over a million visitors to the Zoo in 1965-66, the opening of the Children's Zoo in 1966, the opening of the giraffe house in 1967, and the first-ever concerted membership drive in 1969, funding continued to be a problem for the zoo.

After years of talk and hand wringing, April 1973 saw the first admission fees at the gates of the Buffalo Zoo. $1 for adults, 35 cents for children 6-16, under 6 were free. The budget surpassed $1 million for the first time in 1974.

So just as Parkside struggled through much of the second half of 20th century, so, too, did the Zoo. There were highlights and low lights along the way. Parkside joined the rest of Buffalo in catching "Koala Fever" when in summer 1987, Blinky Bill, the Australian Koala, was expected to attract more that 200,000 people to the Zoo and the neighborhood for the month he was on display.

But for the most part, as a community, Parksiders seemed more interested with the Zoo's exterior maintenance than what was going on inside the cages. In the spring of 1991, The Buffalo Zoo unveiled plans for a new Parkside/Russell entrance, an expansion of the elephant display, and an education department building, the back of which would face mostly Parkside Avenue. As many residents saw it, the planned "improvements" would look like nothing more than a 160-foot long, 12 foot high, concrete wall facing into their neighborhood. After resistance from residents, the height was scaled down to 9 feet, and Zoo officials worked with the community to make the design more aesthetically pleasing to the surrounding community.

As this was being treated as the front page headline story in the *Parkside News*, inside the pages of the community newsletter was an editorial by Friends of Olmsted Parks, suggesting that as the zoo, and its original mandates grew, that it would perhaps be best for the zoo to find a "better location to fulfill its mission."

The writers pointed to the on-going strife over the construction project as an example of how the zoo might be out growing the neighborhood and the park. This was the first mention of a topic that would divide the Parkside Community as the 1990s wore on.

The neighborhood's oldest institution would become its most controversial. Parkside's mettle was tested, when, in 1997, Zoo officials began talk of moving the Zoo from the only home it's ever known in Parkside, to a more open, expansive space near Buffalo's waterfront in the Old First Ward.

The featured topic at the PCA annual meeting, November 18, 1997, at School 54, was to discuss "the new zoo initiative, and the potential uses for the city-owned space currently occupied by the zoo."

Something needed to be done with the aging zoo. As reported in the *Parkside News*, "The decision of the zoo's board to directors to pursue building a new zoo elsewhere in the city, presumably on the waterfront, has been widely reported. The zoo faces the probability of losing its accreditation without major investments to modernize animal habitats and make other mandated changes.

"(Zoo Director Tom) Garlock explained.... Space limitations at the existing site, both for modernizing existing habitats and increasing parking space; and a lack of funding sources for zoo renovation also played a role in the board's decision to pursue a new site."

Many residents were angered by the Zoo Board's later admission that they never seriously considered staying in Delaware Park. In a February, 1998 letter to Buffalo Mayor Anthony Masiello, PCA President George Stock wrote regarding the plans to move the Zoo:

> *"We have been disappointed and a bit mystified by the seeming lack of interest on the city's part concerning this dramatic development in our neighborhood, which poses the most significant challenge to Parkside's stability in recent history.*
>
> *"While divided over whether the Zoo should stay or move, our residents are of one mind on the necessity for the city to begin working with our neighborhood now to address the implications of the situation.*
>
> *"The Zoo's departure would have a stunning impact on our neighborhood... (R)esidents express a sense of deep personal loss, and in some cases, anger, at the Zoo's determination to move. It has been a stalwart, albeit at times controversial, anchor in Parkside for nearly a century. Its departure, no matter what takes its place, would be traumatic and difficult for this stable and prosperous neighborhood."*

Numerous meetings were held between residents, the Zoo, and city officials. Mayor Masiello had created a Zoo-Re-Use task force. Many neighbors felt their world turned upside down as they had barely been able to celebrate the progress being made in revitalizing the Darwin Martin House, as they began another uphill fight to save another neighborhood landmark.

It was a grassroots effort built up over decades that helped save the Martin House. Any efforts to keep the Zoo put would have to gain critical mass in a much more expedient fashion. A half-dozen neighbors sitting in a Woodward Avenue living room were struck with an inspiration, some money was quickly collected from the group, and The Committee to Keep the Zoo in Delaware Park was born.

The committee spread hundreds of lawn signs reading *Improve, Don't Move*. They only counted one "lonely" "New Zoo Now" sign in Parkside. Janice Barber and Joel Rose wrote in the *Parkside News*, the disparity "stand(s) as a silent testament to the sentiment of most Parkside residents."

The signs became a phenomenon, and spread around the region like wild fire. Clarence, Elma, Niagara County; one was hard pressed to find a community where there wasn't a home showing support for keeping the Zoo in the space place where it had entertained and educated since 1875.

As the debate intensified, there were several reports of mass theft of "Improve Don't Move" signs. One witness told of three men in a black pickup truck stripping several blocks of Crescent and Summit Avenues of the signs in the early morning hours of a single day. A week later, other blocks of Crescent and Woodward were hit.

Meanwhile, Zoo officials were doing what they thought would be in the best interest of the animals. They thought a new facility would help re-ignite their fundraising, which had fallen off dramatically, making refurbishing the aging Parkside campus exceedingly difficult. Zoo President Thomas Garlock publicly stated on numerous occasions that he felt it was the selfish desire of home owners to protect property values, and not the best interest of the animals, motivating those fighting to move the zoo to a property more than three times the size of the Parkside facility (80 acres vs. 24 acres).

Though he later admitted the comment was "curt and off the cuff," Garlock did little to soothe things over with the *anti-moving crowd* when he was widely quoted as saying, "The only animals the people in the Parkside neighborhood are concerned about are the homo sapiens."

In fall 1998, The Zoo Board voted to move forward with plans to secure $160 million in funding for a new Zoo and aquarium on Buffalo's waterfront, three blocks from then-Marine Midland Arena. Wide public opinion, gauged through polls, calls, and letters, prompted officials to seek government funding on all levels for the project.

The issue was much bigger than just the neighborhood, and made some strange bedfellows. Some Parksiders who'd spent 16 years fighting with Jimmy Griffin as Mayor, suddenly found him as an ally in the *Move the Zoo* debate. Griffin was upset at the proposal's reliance on public money, and thought the waterfront deserved better, telling reporters, "I know we've always had an awful lot of wildlife down in the First Ward, and I was part of it," Griffin laughed. "But this is outrageous." But the region as a whole was split. A *Business First* poll conducted by Goldhaber Research in August/September 1998 showed that 43% of Western New York residents wanted to see the Zoo move, and 43% wanted to see the Zoo renovate the existing facility.

The neighborhood and the PCA galvanized in opposition to the Zoo's Board's plans to not only move, but its plans to seek millions in public funding to build the new, $250 million zoo. Despite Zoo officials insistance that the move was a "done deal," the thousands of "Improve, Don't Move The Zoo" lawn signs, and the spirit behind them helped keep the venerable institution at its Parkside home.

Of all the opinions that were offered over the year-and-a-half battle, the most important one, however, came from someone who'd never been to the Zoo, and only to Parkside once or twice. New York Governor George Pataki was reluctant to provide any funding for the waterfront project, and within days, both candidates for Erie County Executive, Joel Giambra and Dennis Gorski made clear they couldn't support the project without the financial support of the Governor.

18 months of gut-wrenching neighborhood controversy ended when Zoo Directors voted in September 1999 to remain at the Parkside location. The whole affair was akin to a Civil War in the neighborhood, and many neighbors still maintain icy relationships after tempers flared and tactics were challenged as the question of moving the zoo boiled. Garlock quit the Zoo, and he was replaced in September 2000 with Donna Fernandes. Her ability to spearhead the raising of a record $24 million for improving the Buffalo Zoo was no doubt made easier, ironically, by her predecessor's very public failure in trying to move the facility.

After the decision to improve was made, millions of dollars worth of renovations were realized, with much expected in the future. Now one of the more popular attractions, the Sea Lion Exhibit opened in 2005, proving the Zoo didn't have to be moved, and could be improved. The exhibit also welcomed one of the neighborhood's more verbose residents to the area. The loud and joyful barks of Smokey the Sea Lion resonate throughout the neighborhood, and are the sounds that many Parksiders fall asleep to with their windows open summer evenings.

Delaware Park: Again a Source of Pride

When Frederick Law Olmsted designed *The Park*, replete with *The Meadow*, it wasn't too long thereafter that *The Deer Paddock* was added, soon to become the Zoo. And almost since the beginning, there's been tension between the Park and the Zoo.

A 1978 Zoo masterplan called for a 500 car parking lot in the middle of the Delaware Park Meadow. Outraged residents spoke up, but the Zoo still insisted upon (and received) a new entrance along Ring Road, complete with snack bar and gift shop looking out over the ball diamonds and rugby fields the planners had earlier hoped to pave over.

Mark Goldman writes in his 1983 book *High Hope:, The Rise and Fall of Buffalo, NY* that "the city went along with the zoo, and this once safe and quiet park area has become traffic-clogged, dangerous, and unsightly. Thus, Delaware Park remains fair game for road happy planners and a car crazed public."

As late as 2000, in the wake of the *Move the Zoo* controversy, once it was decided the Zoo would stay put, a plan was floated to expand the Zoo's footprint into the area of the park between Ring Road and Parkside Avenue, replacing the basketball courts and tot lot with parking. The plan was quickly abandoned.

It wasn't just Zoo interests that impeded residents from using the park to its fullest, poor planning, or battling interests often left park users less than satisfied. Through the years, a lack of sanitation and gardening, battles between golfers trying to play through the baseball outfields, and outfielders dodging sliced tee shots, and the ever increasing presence of the automobile left many to wonder whether it was worth visiting the park.

Much of the 1980s was spent with Parksiders debating the merits of vehicular traffic on Meadow Road (the "Ring Road" in Delaware Park.) At one point, one could circumnavigate the entire park via automobile, and many did so with little regard to the safety of those making use of the park. While the open road made the ball diamonds, golf course, and soccer fields more accessible, it also encouraged use of the park as a cut through. It was a hotly debated topic in Parkside, with some saying cutting off park traffic will clog neighborhood streets, and others wishing autos to be banned nearly completely from the park. Resident David Gerber lamented the condition of Delaware Park in a March/April 1988 op-ed piece in *The Parkside News*:

> *Our various attachments to the park have deepened the sadness many of us have felt, especially over the last five or so years, over problems that seem to pervade Delaware Park. Automobiles compete with bike riders, bike racers, runners, walkers, wheel chair exercisers, and even the occasional big wheel driver for use of the traffic laden Ring Road. Golf, soccer, and baseball vie for the same space, each menacing in different ways to the others. Volleyball can only be played along the frequently flooded bridal path. There seems no longer to be a place to sit and have a picnic or simply enjoy the open space, grass and trees.*
>
> *There isn't enough room for parking, and the Zoo threatens from time-to-time to grab what room there is. The Park doesn't seem safe for family recreation. It's growing less enticing for everyone, a victim of its own attractiveness, and of a fierce competition for space that seems to have no rules but the survival of the strongest.*

After years of public debate, Acting Parks Commissioner Stan Buczkowski favored a plan closing Ring Road to traffic, saying it was the only way to calm traffic, especially with only two police officers assigned to the entire city parks system at the time. By fall of 1990, Buczkowski oversaw the installation of the permanent barriers on Ring Road at the Middlesex Road entrance. Traffic almost immediately dropped to a trickle.

Often throughout the 135 year history of Buffalo's parks, tough economic times have left the public spaces in desperate need of repairs and attention. However, through budget crises of the 1990s and 2000s that left the City of Buffalo and Erie County under the fiscal screws of two separate Fiscal Control Authorities, Buffalo's Parks *actually came out ahead*. The result was an historic agreement with the Olmsted Parks Conservancy.

Guided by the original plans of Frederick Law Olmsted for an "urban landscape that integrates the city, providing common ground and connectivity among the neighborhoods," the conservancy has fought for respect for the parks. Heavily involved in the push to have speed reduced on the Scajaquada Expressway, the most noticeable difference in Delaware Park for most Parksiders since Olmsted's taking it over-- The beautiful gardens that have replaced the dried out mud patches along the park's borders with the community.

It's a Renaissance that has certainly been noticed by longtime residents of the Parkside area. George Zornick, who grew up on Russell Avenue in the 1960s and 70s, now lives on Parkside Avenue directly across from the Park. He greatly appreciates the difference. "The park is so much better kept now; so much more beautiful. Back when the city owned it, they mowed the grass and that was about it; the golf course was ragged. I don't want to say it was scattered with litter, but it's not like today with the zone gardeners and everything is so nice and manicured."

Though at press time of this work the future of the agreement between the Olmsted Conservancy and the City of Buffalo remains unclear, the Olmsted folks remain committed to dozens of $1 million-plus projects around Delaware Park over the next 20 years, including an $80.3 million casino restoration, a $10.2 million Hoyt lake restoration/renovation, a $908,000 renovation of the meadow area, a $4.09 million renovation of baseball diamonds, a $954,000 Parkside Lodge restoration, and a $9.47 million reconstruction of Ring Road.

Perhaps the biggest plans to help recapture the original essence of Frederick Law Olmsted involve the Conservancy's leadership on plans to down grade the Scajaquada Expressway back into a parkway over the next 2 decades, at an estimated cost of $33.7 million.

National Treasure: The Darwin Martin House Renewed

When Frank Lloyd Wright inscribed a copy of his autobiography to Darwin and Isabelle Martin in 1932, he did so with a dramatic flourish, sending their way the sort of praise he usually only lavished on his own work:" *To Darwin D. Martin and his wife—hero and heroine of this tale—with esteem, affection and gratitude from their architect – Frank Lloyd Wright."*

The inscription juxtaposes wonderfully with a note written to Sebastian Tauriello, the Buffalo architect who bought the nearly 20-year abandoned Darwin Martin House on Jewett Parkway in 1954. The home had been sacked by vandals, neighborhood children, and by the son of the original owner Darwin D. Martin, Darwin R. Martin. Tauriello thought having a copy of the original plans of the home might help him in the almost insurmountable task of bringing new life to the home that Wright called "The Opus." He wrote to the by-then aged Martin, who no doubt knew of the condition of the home, and the massive efforts about to be undertaken to breathe new life into his worn masterpiece. Wright's response was frosty at best:

> *Dear "Tauriello": Hope you treat the opus according to its merits. When we return to Wisconsin May first I will look up the plans and send you a set of prints with a bill for the prints.*

Uncertain of what a bill from an eccentric Frank Lloyd Wright might be, the Tauriello family proceeded without the plans.

As "the opus" sat in a state of disrepair, rotting, several individuals and organizations made attempts to salvage and save the house from the time it was abandoned by the Martin family in 1937. The Buffalo Philharmonic Orchestra tried, unsuccessfully, to raise funds to buy the home. The City, which bought the home for $394.53, did so when it was auctioned for taxes in 1946.

In 1952, the city swapped properties with Patrick Dwyer. The city wanted to build a school on land Dwyer had owned elsewhere in the city, and Dwyer immediately started plans to raze the entire Martin complex, including the main home, to make way for an apartment building. Neighborhood outcry, more concerned about property values than the possibility of losing an architectural treasure, quickly ended those plans.

Driving along Jewett Parkway one day, Sebastian Tauriello became interested in the Martin House after seeing the "For Sale" sign planted in the yard by Dwyer. The successful Buffalo architect, who lived with his family on Amherst Street, was well aware that the home was built as the finest, most complete example of Wright's Prairie Style. But by 1954, it was a decrepit eyesore that that been sold for taxes eight years earlier, and was known as a place for adventuresome neighborhood kids to climb inside and find "stuff" (albeit *Frank Lloyd Wright designed* "stuff") to smash and break.

The home itself was assessed at $0, because of the severe damage the structure had endured. The property was assessed at $22,000, and that's what the Tauriello family paid for the house, pergola, conservatory, and garage in April 1954.

Mortgages of $35,000 were taken out to begin the process of turning the crumbling edifice into a home. The sprawling main house was divided into a living space for the Tauriello family, an office for his architecture business, and two other apartments. One of the apartments was occupied by 1930s Buffalo radio star and later WBEN-TV Station Manager George Torge for virtually the entire time the family owned the home.

Darwin Martin House, 1965. The sign reads "Jewett Gardens."

In order to afford the massive undertaking, the Tauriello family had, from the beginning, planned to sell most of the two acres of land that came with the house. These plans were realized in 1960, when Tauriello had the severely damaged pergola, conservatory and garage demolished to make the land desirable to buyers. Unlike the attempts almost a decade earlier to build apartment buildings on the property, neighbors seemed accepting of plans given the tremendous amount of work that had been poured into the property.

Three apartment buildings were constructed in the backyard of the Martin House, two stories high, holding a total of 20 units. Dubbed *The Jewett Gardens*, the construction isolated the three remaining structures of the original Martin complex: The Martin House, the Barton House, and the Gardener's Cottage.

Sebastian & Ruth Tauriello and family saw through renovations to the Martin House to shore it up, and make it a home befitting their own tastes. Their efforts almost certainly saved a neighborhood landmark from continued decay and worse. Sebastian Tauriello died in 1965, and in 1967, UB President Martin Meyerson had the University purchase the home as the President's Residence. The UB School of Architecture endeavored to make sure that Buffalo and the world knew what a treasure stood at the corner of

View of apartments from Woodward Avenue. Built 1960, torn down 2003. Note also the Parkside purchased Streng Olds in the driveway. Bernard Wagner photo.

Jewett Parkway and Summit Avenue, made much easier with the growing appreciation of Frank Lloyd Wright, and particularly his Prairie style.

Eventually, the home no longer fit in SUNY plans, and, in 1980, neighbors were worried as UB was about to hand the home over to the state for disposition. The PCA was very concerned that the house remain in public hands and that it be available for tours. That concern grew into an effort that had the house designated as a National Historic Landmark in 1986. Martin House Curator John O'Hern told the *Buffalo News* at the time of the designation, "This brings attention to the fact that the building has national significance, and not just local significance. Sometimes we need to be reminded by somebody outside our area about what we have."

John C. Courtin, a longtime Jewett Avenue resident, served many years as the liaison between the Parkside Community Association and the group coordinating restoration efforts at the Darwin Martin House starting in the 1980s. He also played a vital role in the massive renovation and restoration that's taken place at the complex through the 1990s and 2000s.

The Darwin Martin House Restoration Corporation was officially founded, and a cooperation agreement signed between the group, SUNY Buffalo, and the State Office of Parks, Recreation, and Historic Preservation on March 26, 1993 at the Martin House.

Three phases of complete restoration have taken place. Surrounding lands and homes have been purchased and returned to the way they were in 1907. In a reversal of history, the three large apartment complexes constructed on the grounds in the 1960s were demolished, in order to make way for the rebuild of the Wright designed pergola, conservatory, and carriage house; just as the decrepit 60 year old remnants of the Wright Originals were condemned to make way for the apartment structures.

Governor George Pataki and Senators Hillary Clinton and Charles Schumer were among the dignitaries in attendance as the ribbon was cut on the restored buildings on October 4, 2006. The ribbon was cut by Eric Lloyd Wright and Darwin Martin Foster, the grandsons of the architect and the patron.

The three homes on the Darwin Martin House Complex are only the beginning of the Frank Lloyd Wright/Martin influence in the neighborhood. Martin's first home in Parkside was a Victorian built a block away from the famous complex on Summit Avenue. Wright designed a home for another Larkin Soap Executive, Walter Davidson, on Tillinghast Place. The home above, on the corner of Willowlawn and Crescent, was built for Mrs. Bagnell, the music teacher of the Martin Children. Frank Lloyd Wright actually visited with her, but she was shocked by the price involved. So Emerson Dell, a Wright trainee, designed her home of much more modest materials in the Prairie style.

In 2009, a new visitors' center, The Greatbatch Pavilion, was opened to the public. The $5 million glass enclosed structure was designed by Toshiko Mori.

While the world-renown Wright structures that are a part of the Martin Complex have been in the spotlight and gained worldwide attention for decades, Parkside is also the home of another Wright home that has gone under a transformation in recent years. The Walter V. Davidson House, at 57 Tillinghast Place, was purchased by businessman Russ Maxwell in 2006. He hoped to open the home as an upscale, rentable-by-the night bed-and-breakfast-without-the-breakfast setup, but neighbors verbosely opposed the plan. None the less, the home has received hundreds of thousands of dollars in much needed TLC, paint, and landscaping, and has been opened often for various occasions and events, including the Parkside Tour of Homes.

Parkside Today and Tomorrow

While, like any other city neighborhood, Parkside continues to deal with many of the issues of urban living; Parkside also seems to band together to deal with the problems like few other communities. After a rash of break-ins in 2007, putting many residents on edge, a grass roots e-mail tree grew from the PCA, block clubs, and strong neighborhood friendships. The burglars were caught, due in large measure, to the vigilance and awareness stepped up by the mass e-mails, and the resounding feeling that criminals weren't going to run the neighborhood.

In a front page article in the *Buffalo News*, titled *Parkside Keeps an Eye on What's Going On* (April 27, 2008), Stephen T. Watson writes:

> *Residents of the Parkside neighborhood stay in close contact, let each other know what's going on and quickly report any problems or suspicious activity...There's a kind of a sense of neighborhood awareness and activism.*

In naming Parkside one of the *top city neighborhoods,* a 2003 *Business First* Article says of the neighborhood, "'There's a great community association in Parkside that really gets things done,' says (Realtor Carole) Holcberg. 'They do a house tour; they do a garden walk. They really improve the quality of life there.' Fifty-eight percent of the workers who live in Parkside hold management or professional positions like doctors, lawyers or teachers. Only four other city neighborhoods are above 50 percent."

The reasons are numerous, but growing neighborhood educational institutions like Canisius and Medaille Colleges, Mount St. Joseph's Academy, St. Mark School, Nichols, and St. Mary's School for the Deaf make academics feel at home in the neighborhood.

The numbers of and quality of amenities also continues to grow. During the 1980s, Parksiders lamented that there wasn't a venue to buy fresh produce or meat. While retail in Parkside has remained limited, the surrounding North Buffalo retail scene has exploded. Target and Office Max opened in 1996 in plot of land on Delaware Avenue that was once an old railroad track bed and a junk yard. Wegmans opened in 1997 on land that was once a Mentholatum factory. In 2005, the west side of Delaware Avenue at Linden was a used car dealer, with an abandoned Tops Market and Ames Department store behind it. The area today boasts a IHOP restaurant, Tim Hortons, and Kohl's Department store; all new builds, and a Big Lots store in half of what used to be Tops. Dozens of restaurants, taverns, and boutiques dot *The Hertel Strip*, a shopping and "night out" Mecca for the crowd that likes the nightlife, but not at the fevered pitch found elsewhere in the city.

The Parkside Community Association remains a strong voice in the community. As the feel of the neighborhood has changed, the focus of the group has to some degree as well. Code enforcement is still a high priority, but so, too, has become the celebration of those who prize and want to share their homes and neighborhood with the city and the world. Kathleen Peterson was the Executive Director of the Parkside Community Association from 1998-2009, and saw events like the Parkside Tour of Homes and the Parkside Garden Tour grow into institutions, and become main sources of funding for PCA programs as city, county, state and federal funding became ever more scarce.

The Parkside Sign was erected at the corner of Parkside and Florence in 1998.

There are many individuals who have watched Parkside evolve over the decades. Jack Anthony has been a Parkside observer in parts of eight decades. Some of the zeal of the past is gone, but he says, the people keep the neighborhood moving. "Even today, we still have black people moving into Parkside, and we still have white people moving into Parkside. It's still a rarity in the city. It's wonderful. But the PCA and the various block clubs serve different purposes now. People talk about crime and traffic, which is the same anywhere you go. What do you organize around? We were fighting blockbusting, fighting for our neighborhood. We had a reason to get started. People were scared about blockbusting. It's not like getting people excited about planting flowers. But we are still organized here, ready to go in case something happens."

But you needn't have grown up in Parkside to become a leading citizen. After nearly a decade and a half of shepherding the Good Shepherd flock as the Episcopal Church's Rector, The Rev. David Selzer has become a neighborhood institution. He and his family have played a vital role in the Parkside Community, and most were sad to see them leave Parkside for Ottawa in August, 2008. Before he left, he talked about what he'll miss most about Parkside:

We moved here from the Twin Cities. Our first apprehension was that we were no longer in a big city, Our second apprehension was that we heard from people the stories were all about the good ol' days, that so much of the identity was with the steel plants closing, and that there were just a lot of memories. The nervousness came with, 'Well, is that all Buffalo is?'

Someone kept saying, Buffalo is 'The City of Good Neighbors.' Our experience, in the 13 years we've been here, is that not only is Buffalo the City of Good Neighbors, but its a thriving community, and particularly the Parkside Neighborhood. It's extremely integrated. More integrated than the neighborhood we lived in Minneapolis. It welcomes people of all races, people of all kinds of cultures and backgrounds; it values its history. People are very caring and motivated, too. Whether it be the Buffalo Zoo or the casino, the people here have a tendency to be very active about it, and that's very wonderful thing. People aren't just going to sit by and let history happen to them without creating it.

It's also this neighborhood of incredible history and gift. From the houses that many people live in, to the institutions that are also a part of it. The other gift I see in this neighborhood is that a number of the institutions are willing to work together, for improvement of not just their own particular piece of turf, but the whole community as well.

My sense is community is the most important aspect of living in a neighborhood. I've always been convinced that suburbia is deadly because it isolates people, and that the gift of the city is clearly that sense of being neighbors, and being in community with each other. That can happen through the church, or through community organizations like the PCA, but it has to be planned, and it has to be deliberate. It has to be worked on. What's great here, is that happens, but we're really in danger if we say, 'Oh, it was wonderful, but it's not happening now." You have to keep it moving.

Writing based on a conversation with longtime Parkside activist and past PCA President Ruth Lampe, Mark Goldman wrote succinctly about the neighborhood in his 2007 book *City on the Edge*:

Because of the proximity to Main Street, near both Cansius College and the old campus of the University of Buffalo, Parkside's reasonably priced Victorian homes have long attracted the local academics. Parkside also attracted upwardly mobile, second- and third-generation ethnics particularly Irish Americans. When block-busting realtors, hoping to prey on the fears of white residents of Parkside, began hovering around the neighborhood in the 1960s, a handful of concerned neighborhood activists, eager to defend their community against the tactics that had destroyed so many others, organized the Parkside Community Association... though blacks were moving into the neighborhood in increasing numbers, the whites of Parkside, encouraged by the work of their community association, stayed. By the end of the decade, a time when so many other neighborhoods succumbed to the frightening cycle of events that caused blight and decline, Parkside not only survived but thrived as a racially mixed, inspiringly beautiful middle-class neighborhood in the heart of the city.

As Parkside looks to the future, it looks to the past to pave that road ahead. The rebuilt Martin House Complex brings thousands to Buffalo and Parkside each year. Historians like George Stock organize and give walking tours of the neighborhood to eager Buffalonians unaware of the architectural treasurers lurking in the *neighborhood by the zoo*. It's the same effect when the PCA sponsors its annual Tour of Homes.

History is being remembered and preserved, as folks like Michael Riester and Patrick Kavanagh, in 2000, organized efforts to place a marker on

Main Street near Humboldt, in memory of the sacrifices made at Flint Hill during the War of 1812, 200 years ago. Nearly 60 folks attended the unveiling, including Mrs. Ruth Granger Zelanek , the great-granddaughter of Judge Erastus Granger. A volley of taps was played in memory of the lives lost during the War of 1812, and those several hundred in the Parkside neighborhood.

Riester and Mike O'Sullivan, both past Presidents of the Parkside Community Association, have researched the provenance of virtually every home in the neighborhood for the PCA's Century Plaque Program, which recognizes homes that have made it through 100 years still in one piece.

Michael Riester is one of many residents who've made a life of collecting and preserving the history of Parkside, while at the same time shaping its future. Pictured here in 1977, Mike wrote and edited a Parkside History brochure, the first attempt at collecting the history of the area in a single publication.

Finally, a quote from the tireless Ruth Lampe, a transplant from Iowa who has helped drive Parkside in the right direction for four decades. "PCA used to be an activist organization with basic concern for immediate community problems. We became, necessarily, involved in government grants and programs. Now those grants are coming to an end. PCA is at a cross roads. I hope that it can revitalize itself and again look to zoning issues and the problems of residents. PCA has gone through many phases in its short history. I'm confident it will find its role. But it takes people with the energy to involve themselves in community affairs." Ruth said that in 1984, but it's just as true today. Hopefully, the readers of this book will take to heart those words, and help make the places they live, where ever they may be, better places to live.

About the Author

Steve Cichon is an award winning journalist with WBEN Radio, where he's been a news reporter and anchor since 2003, having worked in Buffalo radio and television since 1993.

Steve and his wife Monica became Parkside home owners on Valentines Day 2000, and quickly fell in love with the neighborhood. They continue to renovate and restore their 1909 EB Green designed American Four Square, and will likely continue to do so into perpetuity.

Both Steve and Monica have served on the Parkside Community Association Board of Directors, and both are very active in community events, like the Parkside Home and Garden Tours. Steve also serves as a lector at St. Mark Roman Catholic Church, where they were married (*below, on the steps of St. Marks, 2001*). Though it didn't make the first 168 pages of this tome, Steve believes his wedding day to be the greatest day in Parkside History.

While obviously Steve has an interest in the history of Parkside, that interest extends to the history of all of Buffalo, and Western New York as well. He's the curator, writer, and webmaster at *staffannouncer.com*, a website dedicated to preserving and sharing the Buffalo area's pop culture history, particularly the history of Buffalo radio and television. Steve is the past President of the Buffalo Broadcast Pioneers, a non-profit group dedicated to preserving the area's broadcasting history.

Steve is a firm believer that while most people might say they find "history" boring; everyone enjoys a good story-- particularly if it helps tell the person listening to it *how they got where they are.*

Thanks....

To all of those dozens of people; scholars, journalists, and historians, who've collected and written individual portions of this history over the years, and left it waiting for me to find and collect here; among them, Michael Riester, George Stock, Barton Atkins, Ellen Parisi, Marjorie Quinlan, Frank Severance, Mark Goldman, Chuck LaChiusa, Pat Kavanagh, Art Lalonde, Jim Powell, Steve Powell, Donald Norton, and many others.

Also to the many, many individuals who shared their stories and historical ephemera and photos with me for inclusion in this book; Including: Jack Anthony, Michael Riester, Bernie Wagner, George Stock, Ann Marie Flett, George Zornick, Greg Lodinsky, Jan Barber, Ruth Lampe, Len Mattie, Paul Crowley, Pamela Rohring, Jennifer Fields, Tom Burns, Sr. Gail Glenn, Al Tinney, Carl Schmitter, Al Wallack, Fred Kerr, Al Kerr, Sam Hoyt, Kevin Keenan, Aaron Heverin, Msgr. Francis Braun, Rev. David Selzer, John Bisci, Tom Malamas, Dan Ryan, Al Villa, Bob Venneman, Chief Dennis Richards, Chief Charles Fieramusca, Marsha Henderson, Joe Crangle, and many, many others.

And there were also many Parkside friends and neighbors who lent vital moral support over the 19 months this project dragged on (i.e., listened to me drone on about it.) Among them: David Lampe, Tom Ziobro, Mike O'Sullivan, Jack O'Sullivan, Rich Wolf, Pat Lalonde, Chris Lavey, Tom Dolan, Marlene Smith-Amaker, Bob Barends, James Rusk, Randy Bushover, Nancy Abramo, John Warner, Amy Dembski, Kelly Barbus, Kathy Peterson, Diane Kasting, Paula Dolega, Vanessa Currie and too many others. Thanks for your patience.

Special Thanks to Brian Meyer for his invaluable expert advice; Marty Biniasz for being a partner in history and sharing history; Michael Riester for being the Godfather of this project and infecting me with his contagious life-long love of Parkside; and my family: Greg, Lynne, Stephen, and Melissa & Jim, Mom and Dad, Mom and Dad H., Jim and Pat, Amanda and Catherine, Haley, the best grandparents anyone could ever ask for, and most of all, my wife Monica—who gave up her husband for too much time during the course of putting this book together. Thanks Sweetie Pie, *I love ya......*

All images in this volume are either from the Parkside Community Association Archives or from the author's personal collection unless otherwise noted.

This book marks Staffannouncer.com's first foray into the publishing world.

Initially created as a website to share Steve's thousands of images and sounds from Buffalo's radio and TV past, staffannouncer.com has grown to become an online celebration of Buffalo's pop-culture history, devoted to bringing to the World Wide Web the people, places and thoughts of Buffalo that you won't find anywhere else on the internet, and its all done with Steve's sense of history and sense of humor.

Over half a million visitors have enjoyed Steve's virtual strolls down Buffalo's memory lane since 2003.

COPIES OF THIS BOOK, INCLUDING BULK ORDERS, CAN BE PURCHASED AT *STAFFANNOUNCER.COM*

Proceeds from the sale of this book are benefiting various non-profit groups of Parkside, including the Parkside Community Association, St. Mark Roman Catholic Church, and the Episcopal Church of the Good Shepherd.

Made in the USA
Middletown, DE
26 September 2020